MORE TO ORGANISING

How to Help Your Child Become
More Independent and Make Your Life Easier by
Organising With Your Child in Mind

Kathryn Lord

10-10-10
Publishing

This book is dedicated to you, the reader!

I see you. You are busy, and I understand.
I know what it is like to have little hands in every container,
and little hungry mouths needing to be fed.
Why are there not enough hours in the day?
Why is there so much to do?

I promise that things don't have to be so difficult.
By empowering your little ones to be more independent
and helpful around the house, and by decluttering and
organising, you can make your life easier, save time by
knowing and seeing where things are, and have fewer things
that waste your time.

Organising with your child in mind will make them more
autonomous and independent, freeing them to be able to play
and develop more easily. Instead of spending time constantly
tidying up, enjoy your time with your little ones.

Love Kat @more_to_organising

Table of Contents

Foreword

When I first met Kat, I was in awe! Here was a young woman whose passion for her work, first as a teacher and then as a supernanny and author, had taken her around the world and brought magic into the lives of children and families wherever she went.

My background was altogether different. With almost 30 years' experience of the elements now known as 'Interiors Therapy'– decluttering, life coaching, Feng Shui, supportive use of space, organising, gratitude, positive thinking and helping clients gain clarity about the impact and overwhelm possessions can cause for individuals, families and relationships–it didn't seem Kat and I had much in common. Nevertheless, we totally connected.

Soon afterwards Kat booked her first Interiors Therapy session. Despite her exciting lifestyle, she realised something was holding her back from achieving more, and she was determined to deal with it. Little did we know this was the beginning of a whole new life!

Since then, as her success has grown, Kat has asked me to work with her on each new (larger and more desirable) home. I've seen her go from strength to strength, absorbing and using Interiors Therapy for her own space, and now combining the inspiration of Interiors Therapy with her professional experience into the homes of her nanny families and 'More to Organising' clients.

In this wonderful new book, Kat has written an accessible and deliciously user-friendly guide to revitalising any areas of a home used by children.

I've known clients recoup 30-60 valuable minutes in their mornings simply by taking control of their home and possessions, organising and fine-tuning everything to serve their needs. Kat has taken this to a new level for younger members of the family, and these habits will stay with them as they grow up–making your life easier as well as theirs!

Whether you read *More to Organising* as a nanny or a parent, you'll find the magic within this book to create and organise spaces in which your children can thrive whilst giving you room to breathe and time to enjoy being with them.

Suzanne Roynon
Interiors Therapy Expert, Speaker and Author of *Welcome Home, How Stuff Makes or Breaks your Relationship.*

Chapter 1

Introduction

1

When I was a teen, if you had told my parents that I, their daughter, would open an organising business and write a book on it, they would never have believed you. How did I get here? It would be fair to say I have had many jobs that have helped me become better, such as stocking shelves in Clarks, The Body Shop, and Marks and Spencer's Food during my time at the University of York. It has to be said that trying to fit your whole life in one room, in a flat share in London, will do wonders for decluttering and utilising space more effectively.

Being organised in my job as a teacher and a nanny has helped me make spaces that are easier for children to use more effectively. Looking after three children of different ages in many different nanny roles, and also helping families move house, as well as moving myself into studio flats and finally into my one-bed apartment, means I have gotten better and better.

I haven't done this journey alone. The amazing Suzanne Roynon (author of *Welcome Home, How Stuff Makes or Breaks Your Relationship* and the UK's leading interior's therapist), who I met quite by chance when we both volunteered at an event, has become my mentor and rock through good times and bad. She has helped me declutter my personal space and my mind, which has done wonders for my own path. Getting good support is essential.

I am already the award-winning author of *There's More to Books than Reading – How to Help Your Child Bring Stories to Life,* and I am a speaker at events such as Nannypalooza, the International Nanny Training Day, and the Childcare and Education Expo, as well as the Great British Nanny Conference, which will be in New York in April

2022, where I help parents and nannies bring learning to life through books.

"More to Organising" was opened in November 2021, a year after I joked to an employer that I would give up nannying to become a professional organiser—never a truer word was said in jest, hey? I haven't given up nannying, but I have started to support more families to make their lives easier by decluttering and organising with their children in mind.

This book is going to take you through the areas of development, much like my first book, but instead of sharing books and activities, I will share how to organise those spaces more effectively to help your child to use the space more independently, to find things more easily but also to put things away more easily, and to help you organise and declutter all the spaces in your home that have children's items, to make your life easier. It isn't just about organising space though. It is organising your day, organising your meals, and organising your life so that you can live it to its fullest, with your children.

There will also be anecdotes from my life, which have led me to try and find a better, more organised solution. I have made the mistakes so that you don't have to, which will hopefully make your life easier. I'd love to hear your stories too. Let me know on Instagram @more_to_organising, or join my Facebook community, More to Books, where I share about books and organisation, with your child in mind, to bring learning to life.

A note on organising, when I am placing something or tidying, I have these words playing over and over: "What makes sense?" Funnily enough, common sense is not common. Different families have different things that are important to them. The way to help you live an easier life is to organise your home with your family's needs at the forefront of your mind. One nanny family I started working with had their cups at the other side of the kitchen to where the kettle was, and the mum said, "We put them here when we moved in, and to this day, I still open the wrong cupboard." I have helped them switch the cups with the glasses.

What a family with babies and toddlers needs, will be different to ones who have teenagers. I know it sounds obvious, but I have been in houses where they still have plastic plates and cutlery, but their children have grown and no longer want to use these items. They just become clutter.

I understand and appreciate how difficult it is to get rid of items that have emotional attachment, and I have some ideas to help you with those as well. Check out Chapter Seven.

The chapters in this book can be dipped in and out of. Read what is most relevant to you first. Many principles and themes will be similar throughout each chapter. I really do advocate colour coordination at all times (just like *The Home Edit* does). While I will not be asking you to thank all your items, like Marie Kondo, I do think there is a lot to be said about keeping items that are useful and bring you joy. And I love seeing before and after pictures, just like Stacey Solomon's *Tap to Tidy*, so when this book inspires you to sort out that drawer or shelf or cupboard, please do share to Instagram, linking me @more_to_ organising, and use the hashtag #moretoorganising.

If you would like extra help, check out my online course or get in touch, and I can help you organise with your child in mind.

ACTION

What times of the day are the most stressful?

Allocate these areas, from 1 being most and 6 being least. Go to those chapters in that order.

- Books
- Toys
- Craft
- Clothes
- Bathroom
- Kitchen

Don't try and do everything at once. This is a marathon, not a sprint. Do little by little to make it achievable.

Oh, and always take before and after photos, and post on Instagram @more_to_organising #moretoorganising, or on the Facebook page, More to Books.

Notes

Notes

Chapter 2

Reading Area

2

If you are lucky enough to have a space in your playroom, then that's brilliant! If not, can you make a place in the living room or bedroom? Make a cosy corner using cushions and blankets, an area that you can climb into with your child. It doesn't have to cost lots of money. Use what you already have in your house. Make it with your child. Make it inviting!

Make the corner enclosed by turning your bookshelf into a "three-walled" space. For safety, put another shelving unit or bookcase behind. That way, they will lean on each other to keep upright. As a teacher, it was imperative to teach the children not to climb the bookshelves as they might topple over. If you are concerned, don't position them this way. Most can be screwed to the wall if necessary. If you don't have a bookshelf, the books can be stored in baskets, especially for small children. (I've plagiarised myself from my first book, but I stand by it.)

"What makes sense?"

When it comes to little children—well, all children, and adults—they have to be able to reach them. I was decluttering a 9-year-old's bedroom, and all her books were on the top shelf of the bookshelf, which was kept on top of a chest of drawers. It was a very clever use of space as it was a small room; however, I couldn't even reach these books. Now, I know I am small—five foot three (and a half) (the half is important)—but I am taller than a 9-year-old, and if I can't reach, she can't reach.

In one family, I had a 2-year-old, a 6-year-old, and a 9-year-old. I put the toddler books on the bottom shelf, the middle child's on the middle shelves, and the eldest on the top shelves. Obviously, they can read whichever ones they want, but it was rare that the eldest wanted a toddler book and vice versa; although it is so lovely when they read to each other.

Colour Coordinating

I am going to be talking about this a lot and in many areas, but it just makes sense for children. Ask them what their favourite book is. I bet you they know what colour it is. Even toddlers who can't read know what colour the cover of their favourite book is. There are so many reasons to colour coordinate everything; one being that it just looks so pretty. It actually makes my heart sing. So, if your child knows what colour their favourite book is, they can find it without having to pull out ALL the books on that shelf. I have been there. But guess what? If they are all colour coordinated, your child knows where to put it back too.

Rotation

Some books are so loved, they will never be rotated, and that's fine. As a teacher, learning is based on topics. If you have read my first book, you'll know that I love to use a book as a hook for learning in all areas. So, if your child is showing excitement about a particular topic, pull out all those books based on that topic. Store ones that are not relevant, away in a cupboard, and bring them out another time. This helps for a couple of reasons: It makes space for books that are relevant, but it also means that when the books that they haven't seen for a little while come back, they suddenly become more exciting to read. I am sure this has happened to you as an adult. You end up shoving a book or a DVD (if you still have those), and it gets hidden. You forget it's there—out of sight, out of mind—but when you see it again, it is way more appealing than if it had sat there in plain sight.

Seasonal

I will talk about this again in Chapter Six, "People and Communities." It's still all about rotation. Christmas books and Christmas DVDs (if you still have those) do not need to come out until after you have read and/or watched *The Nightmare Before Christmas*. Them's the rules in my house. Perhaps after bonfire night, then BAM, CHRISTMAS EVERYWHERE. But when it's not the right season, put them away in a labelled box, and don't forget where you put it. It's not just Christmas; there are many books about different seasons, which don't need to be out, such as summer in winter, etc.

Library Books

Please use your local library. I love getting children a library card. My last nanny child didn't have one, and we went together. The child got to choose the picture on the card. I think it really is the key to many worlds. Wimbledon Library just had a revamp, and it's beautiful. Many libraries have story and song time. Encouraging a love of books and reading for pleasure is so important to your child's development. Reading is a prerequisite for most other subjects—if they can be self-motivated to read, half the battle is won for them. Even before being able to learn phonics, segmenting and blending and sight-reading tricky words, learning to hold a book (the right way), and turning the pages and using vocabulary to describe what is happening in the pictures, all helps them.

Reading to your child, even when they are able to read themselves, models the pronunciation of words. When I was eleven (until the films came out), I pronounced Hermione as "her-me-own," because I had never seen that name before. But also, you reading to them will help them listen to intonation and different voices when reading speech. What does this have to do with organising, I hear you say? I know, thank you for reminding me. I am just so passionate. (But seriously, going to the library and reading to them will help them be more independent learners when they are older.)

Once, over the weekend, the library books were put away. I almost fainted. Just kidding. They were put away in amongst all the other books, but I spent half an hour searching for these library books. Thank goodness I could remember what they looked like, but if I had colour coordinated them, it would have been so much easier. So, I want your life to be easier. I know they say people learn from their own mistakes, but I am trying to save you time. Keep your library books separate. Not only does this keep them special, but it means they are kept nicer too. Head to www.moretobooks.blog for the blog on organising books, for extra tips to make the process even easier.

ACTION

- Fix broken books.
- Colour coordinate.
- Donate.
- Check underneath and behind the bookshelf.

Don't try and do everything at once. This is a marathon, not a sprint. Do little by little to make it achievable.

Oh, and always take before and after photos and post on Instagram @more_to_organising #moretoorganising, or on the Facebook page, More to Books.

Competition time: Show me your beautiful book cases!

Notes

Notes

Notes

Chapter 3

Toys

3

Understanding the World

I am a nanny. Do you know how many people tell me I just play with children all day? I mean I do, and I love it. But there are reasons we set up activities. If you want in, go and read my other book! Children learn through play. In the EYFS (Early Years Foundation Stage), the document sets out different areas of development for childcare providers to support children in. Nurseries and reception classrooms are set up so that these areas are available in "continuous provision," so that the children have independent access to this learning and development throughout the day.

"Understanding the World" is broken up into The World, People and Communities, and Technology. I have another chapter including "People and Communities," as there is more to it than just in "Toys" (Chapter Six).

Role Play

Your children learn by watching you. A small kitchen is so important for them to internalise the world around them and play by imitating what you do. In one nanny job, while the eldest two were at school, I had a LOT of laundry and ironing to do. The little man in my life (who features heavily in the first book I wrote, as I was writing it when I was his nanny) was 2 when I met him, but he kept growing up. Children seem to keep doing that. Well, after a while, he dropped his afternoon nap, so I could no longer iron while he was sleeping, but I still had all that ironing to do. I used to fill up the washing-up bowl with warm water and bubbles, and he would wash his plastic plates, bowls, and cups. He loved doing that and would be so happily playing while I finished the ironing. When we would go to a lovely playgroup on a Tuesday, he would get all the pretend irons from their well-equipped play kitchen and do the "ironing."

Having foods, pots, and pans can really help them process their learning. In my new nanny job, the little girl always makes me a pretend cup of tea when we get in from the nursery and school run. Interestingly, that's what the parents do for me too (but a real one). She is doing what is being modelled.

What has this got to do with organising? Well, to help your child become more independent, provide them with a small role-play kitchen. We will talk about how to organise the shelves and cupboards in your actual kitchen, in Chapter Five, "Physical Development – Health and Self-Care." Organising the play kitchen can help their development (e.g., sorting the pretend vegetables and fruit). A tip for making it not get out of hand is to declutter.

- **There will be items that have bits missing. Get rid of them.**
- **There will be items that they never play with. Donate or sell them.**
- **There will be items that are broken or tatty. Fix them or put them in the bin.**

Get your child involved in this process. Organising and decluttering are habits. Habits are part of your life. I understand that this might be hard for you at first, but the wonderful news is, if you help your child to get used to this process when they are young, it will be easier for them as they grow up into wonderful adults. Adults that are not held back by their clutter, lead a life of ease as they keep on top of it. It will just be second nature to them.

Dress Up

Rotate! Rotate! Rotate!

Don't keep Halloween costumes out all year. In fact, if you don't have siblings, your child will not fit into that costume next year, and they probably won't even want to wear it. Box up the accessories (they will fit), label the box, and remember where you've put it. I'll remind you again in Chapter Six, "People and Communities," under the subtitle, "Celebrations."

When was the last time you washed those dress-up costumes? Some can't even be washed. Dab them down with a damp cloth and get that Febreze out. Again, unless you have younger siblings, check the size of the costume, and either sell or donate to charity. Colour coordinate those babies. If possible, have a little wardrobe or hanging rack, and keep them separate from their normal clothes. This will hopefully mean they don't insist that they wear that princess dress to play in the muddy puddles. (Remember, I said that some can't even be put in the washing machine—trust me, I have been there already; I am just trying to make your life easier. I should rename the book, *Learn from All My Mistakes So You Don't Have To*.) By not getting mud on the "I can't be put in the washing machine" princess dress, your life will be easier!

I mean, I know where they are coming from—I want to wear a princess dress to the park as well!

Anyhoo, yup, put them somewhere else, so when they are choosing their clothes, the options are easier to clean—just saying. More on how to organise their actual clothes, in Chapter Five, "Physical Development – Health and Self-Care."

Small World

What is "small world?" The farm, the zoo, the train set, the dolls' house, the cars ... you know, all those "TINY BITS THAT END UP EVERYWHERE; AND OH MY GOD, PLEASE DON'T LET ME STAND ON

THEM WITH BARE FEET" toys. The little plastic animals, the metal cars that Kevin would LOVE to use to slow down the Wet Bandits, or the Sticky Bandits, depending on if you prefer *Home Alone 1* or *Home Alone 2*. Can we give a shout out to Kevin's parents? They must have taught him all the tidying tricks, as that house the day after is spotless, almost. (The metal tooth didn't get cleaned up.)

There are tips to organise all these. We need labelled boxes. As teachers in schools, we label our boxes with the words AND the pictures of what is in them. Some children can't read. But all visually unimpaired children can work out pictures. (I am a guide runner in my spare time. I have supported visually impaired runners to run half-marathons in London, and raised thousands of pounds for RNIB —Royal National Institute of Blind People—by running marathons)

So, take a picture of what is in the box, and pop it on the outside. If your child knows what is in the box, it helps them not pull EVERY box out to find what they are looking for. If there is a picture on the outside of the box, then they are more likely to know where to put the toys back.

Rotate the toys. If the toys are always readily available, they will get bored of them and perhaps not play with them. You don't need the zoo and the farm out at the same time. Make your life easier by not having to sort those animals over and over again.

For one of my child's LOL dolls, we had a box with compartments, and it actually became a game for her to separate the heads, the bodies, the shoes, the clothes, and the accessories. She would colour coordinate them. Remember when I said children see what you do and copy. I didn't ask her to do that. She saw me doing it in other areas of her room and was self-motivated to do that herself. It made her play easier. Instead of spending or wasting a lot of time looking for a tiny shoe, when she wanted to dress this doll a certain way, she knew where all the items were. Her play was transformed, she was more independent, and the play was more purposeful. She actually got to use her imagination by acting out storylines rather than looking for that shoe.

There will be inevitable times when they have set up their train set or dolls' house, and it's time to go somewhere or do something else. I have rules about this, a habit to get them into. Of course, all their efforts of setting up should not be dashed, and if it's set up, next time they come to it, the play will be more purposeful; so, in these cases, let them keep it set up. In schools and nurseries, we have things called "tuff spots," and it might be a wise investment if you have the space for it. What I tell my children whom I nanny, is that they can leave out what is set up, but anything around it that is not "in play," needs to be put back in the box. The theory is, if I had to hoover up, and it's not "set up," it would be hoovered away.

For children who are not lucky enough to have a playroom, it is so important that the toys in their bedrooms are not all over the place. In the middle of the night, if they needed the toilet, the toys are a trip hazard. If there was a fire, you definitely would not want any toys on their route to the door. Even if not in a disaster scenario, having a clear floor means they are less likely to hurt themselves (or you yourself), whether the light is on or not. If they don't hurt themselves, your life is easier! Hurrah!

This is a habit you need to teach them. Just like me teaching the pupils in my classroom that climbing up the bookshelf is not safe, leaving toys on the floor is for health and safety. When I was a teacher, I used to do health and safety reconnoitres on places we were going to take the children for class trips. At one farm, I reversed into a hidden/blind spot boulder in the car park. It actually caused £100 in damages, and it failed its MOT as I couldn't get in the boot to get the spare tyre! Well, anyway, I wrote on the health and safety report that the coach should not go into the car park because of that sneaky boulder. I just can't take my health and safety hat off. Even in nanny houses, if I can see a potential hazard, such as wires on the floor, etc., then I sort it, organise it, and declutter it—if I can prevent an accident, then it means we can spend more quality time together doing baking or craft, rather than sorting out bumps and bruises.

I am not saying that you should wrap your children in cotton wool, and definitely, there are things they need to learn for themselves, but if you can organise your home to be a safe environment for them to explore and play, your life will be a little bit easier. Speaking of hazards or injuries, when I was 7, we moved into a new house that had a new fancy hob. My brother told me to touch it "because it wasn't on." It technically wasn't on, but it had just been on, and I burnt all down my hand. I really wish I had been left with a scar, as I would never have let him live it down. Thankfully, there was no lasting damage.

Construction

Constructing is building, so you have your usual plastic suspects, such as Lego and Magnatiles. These are amazing for their creative development, working out what works, working out how to make their structures sturdier, and following patterns and designing things. As with small world, if it's broken, bin it! If they no longer play with it, donate or sell it! If there are some parts that are lost, get rid of the other ones!

Lego plays a huge part in my nanny career. In one family, they had started to build a Disney Castle but then had their kitchen refitted, so the partially built castle and Lego pieces were moved and subsequently lost between the other bits of Lego. During the first lockdown, there was nothing else to do but colour coordinate (yes, I told you I liked colour coordinating) the bricks to find the correct ones for this castle. I am very happy to tell you that with teamwork, and after several hours, we managed to find all the pieces and follow the instructions to finish the Disney Castle. It was not for the faint hearted. I don't actually advise colour coordinating Lego unless it's for that purpose; although it does mean they can now find pieces they want more easily. The best thing for storing (non-colour coordinated) Lego is a drawstring material bag. They have made them for makeup as well, but the medium-sized ones are perfect for undoing the drawstring so that it ends up being a flat circle. You can see all the Lego pieces easily, and then when you want to tidy up, you just pull the drawstring to turn it back into a bag. It makes life so much easier, and children as young as 4 can do that by themselves!

I have since read an article that Lego has amazing customer service and always does everything in their power to get lost pieces replaced. So if a main character is missing, or an integral piece to your build, get in touch with them.

Jigsaws and Board Games

Jigsaws are amazing for children's fine motor skills. Fine-tuning their fine motor skills makes it easier for them to hold pencils and utensils such as scissors or cutlery. When I was a teacher, I did home visits to meet new children who were joining us in reception. Some parents were excited to tell us that their children were amazing at jigsaws, and while it became apparent that they could indeed match the correct piece of the picture into the puzzle, they were doing them on the iPad. I am not a screen-time phobic, but I believe there is a time and a place for the iPad. As a nanny, I know how hard it is for you as a parent to get everything done, with three children and a puppy! But they are to be used alongside and not instead of.

You know those jigsaw boxes that have three puzzles in one? When your children are really little, and it is too difficult for them to sort the puzzle pieces AND do the jigsaw, the first time you do the jigsaw with them, turn it over and put a coloured "Diddi-Dot" (these are little circle stickers) on the back of every piece; then put a different colour on every piece of the second, and another colour on every piece of the third. This makes it visual for them to sort their puzzles, and therefore gives them autonomy and independence, even as young as 2. You can get on with preparing a meal while they are doing something. The Diddi-Dots can be taken off as the child gets more independent, and it makes the puzzles a little bit harder, but they are now old enough for the challenge of knowing which piece goes with which jigsaw.

If you lose a piece, don't fret; just get rid of that jigsaw. Life is too short to worry about it. Pieces go missing. If you do take it to a charity shop, do pop a sticker on the front to say there is a piece missing.

When supporting one family to declutter, all the family board games were in the top cupboard, all hidden away behind some clutter. I swapped them out for things that they didn't need to use as often, such as a sleeping bag and some ice skates, and put them at the bottom of her wardrobe, and I colo... (yup, you know, I coordinated them by colour—it just makes me happy, okay?). Well, now she can see them, she can reach them herself, and she knows where they are. Out of sight, out of mind is fine if you don't want to see them, but if she has friends over, and you're busy—let's say by taking some much-deserved, well-needed quiet time reading a book or watching a television programme—she can now get that out without having to ask for your help. She is more independent, and your life is easier! So, I did write that with a parent in mind, but let it be said: You nannies that are working twelve-hour shifts (or more or less) with no break, deserve a break too. Go get it, tiger!

Any board games or jigsaws that are too young for them, or which they no longer play with, donate or sell. If there are no younger siblings, you don't need them taking up your valuable space. If they have pieces missing and are no longer usable, get rid of them! Actually, before you get rid of them, contact the company as you might be able to buy spare pieces. My mum and I still play Scrabble with a few letters missing; and of course, whoever loses, it's just because of those missing tiles. I need to follow my own advice for this one. I might try to find out which letters are missing, and get replacements for her Christmas present—shhh, don't tell her!

Technology

How much time do you waste looking for a wire that has gone missing? It used to happen all the time in one of my nanny houses. There was a wire in the living room that would mysteriously go missing, and no one would admit to being the one who took it. When they moved house, I found a wire down the side of the bed of the teenager. Perhaps she had forgotten she had taken it? It is expensive for branded ones. By organising your wires and plugs, you can save some time.

I keep getting tripped up on the wire front (not literally!). I went to the Childcare and Education Expo, in Coventry, after the lockdown. (I spoke there before the pandemic!) I have USB plugs in the wall in my apartment, so I just pulled the wire and went on my way. Outside of London, it seems this is not a good idea. I had a wonderful day networking with the lovely people from Thinkably (my first book is on their digital platform) and Yoginis Yoga (I have interviewed both of them for my blog,), only to get to the hotel and find that I should have brought a plug. I promptly turned off my dying phone (my train ticket was on it) and had a lovely relaxing bath while reading a murder mystery—so relaxing! I watched actual terrestrial television, which was so novel, and I fell asleep.

Luckily, the bus back to the Ricoh Centre had a USB socket, so I didn't have to stay there forever, but I imagine that my life would have been easier if I had taken one with me. I am definitely going to learn from it—well, I said I would, but then I went to Yorkshire, to a cottage with my mum, and guess what? I didn't take the plug. My mum had one, so I used it in the day, and she used it overnight. So, from NOW on, I will remember to take my plug—honest.

With one family that I began with, the children were addicted to their iPads. They had them from before I arrived at 7 a.m., and wanted them all evening too. To start with, I got the parents to put a timed lock on them. So, they could have their iPads, but once the time was up, it was locked and behind a password protected part. I then asked their dad to hide them somewhere in the house, working on two principles: out of sight, out of mind—I like that one; can you tell? And also, if I don't know where it is, I can't get them, and I am not lying. I don't like lying to children. I think we should treat them like humans, but also, as an adult myself, it is my responsibility to give them a healthy balance.

Of course, the children tried to look for their iPads, and once or twice they found them; but soon, iPad-filled mornings were transformed into games of Monopoly, and iPad-addicted afternoons turned into baking or craft. I have just babysat them again after a few years. They are both now taller than me, but we baked brownies and played board games just like the old times. So, was that easy? Probably not initially. The parents and I had to work together, and there were tantrums at the beginning, but it was so worth it. We used icing to write their spellings and tricky words on the biscuits and buns we made. I created games where they had sentences with missing words that were hidden around the house. We had movie night on Fridays after swimming. My time with them was fun, and we all have very fond memories. Life was easier when I didn't have to fight with the screen time. I am not against screen time; we even used the iPad to make a stop-start animation, and we made videos of us reading stories. I just like to use screen time in a purposeful and healthy way. It is all about balance.

With a football-loving child, before that family, I used to take videos of him scoring goals in slow-mo, and he would watch them back and improve his technique.

Onto electronic toys and noisy books... Check the batteries in them. There were a number of times when I had been in a nanny family, and either the batteries had just run out, or worse, gone all gunky. You can take the dead batteries to be recycled; most supermarkets have a drop-off for them. Just pop them in a bag labelled "dead," and take them out of your house. For the books, the batteries can be changed. They are usually those tiny, cute batteries. To solve this, I used to take the actual book to the hardware shop to ensure I definitely got the correct size. You will probably need that handy screwdriver you got from that cracker a few years ago—do you remember where it is? If not, check out the chapter on celebrations, in Chapter Six.

So, we have replaced the batteries in our books and toys so that they are now usable, and your child won't ask you, when you're elbow deep in some kind of batter, for those freezable (why isn't freezable a word? It really should be.) blueberry pancake bites (more on those in Chapter Five) ipso facto—your life is a little bit easier, and your child is a little bit more independent. In saying that, as your child gets older, it's a brilliant life skill to be able to change the batteries themselves.

Digital clutter is just as bad as physical clutter. Go through their iPads and delete any apps they no longer use, any from when they were little, and any downloaded cartoons that they no longer need or watch. Organise the apps—you guessed it—with colour coordination. They know what colour the app is, so they can find it more quickly. Do the same for your phone; it will make your life easier—well, until the makers of that particular app do an update and change the colour, which is mildly frustrating. Haha! I do love the feature where you can type the name of the app, and it appears as if my magic, which is great if you can read and write. We want to make your child more independent, so if they cannot read or write yet, they will rely on colour and pictures to help them. One of the stay-at-home mums (SAHM) that I worked alongside, used to let her toddler play on a couple of games while she was in the shower. She didn't want to have to get out the shower to sort the iPad out while dripping wet. See, there is a time and a place for screen time. Make it work for you.

ACTION

Which of these areas caused you the most hassle this week?

Allocate these areas, from 1 being most and 6 being least. Do them in order.

- Role play area
- Dress up
- Small world
- Construction
- Jigsaws and board games
- Technology

Don't try and do everything at once. This is a marathon, not a sprint. Do little by little to make it achievable.

Oh, and always take before and after photos, and post on Instagram @more_to_organising #moretoorganising, or on the Facebook page, More to Books.

Competition time: How many bags did you send to charity? Show me a picture!

Notes

Notes

Chapter 4

Creative Development

Crafty Bits

This bit can end up being the bane of your life if it is not kept on top of. It's the messy play; it's the gunky paints and glues; it's the million tiny pieces of pom poms and beads and pipe cleaners (that never clean pipes). But fear not, I am here to help.

Some things need to be out of reach of your child to make your life easier. We don't want felt tip all over the wall. If that does happen, use toothpaste and a lot of elbow grease. Yes, it's happened to me. Well, it was over the weekend, and it was my fresh hell on a Monday morning. It doesn't have to be that way. Paints, glue, playdough, chalk, and Orbeez—put them up high. That can be an adult-led, or at least an "adult in the vicinity," activity. They only get it again if they tidy up nicely afterwards. It's about teamwork. You are not their slave. Even your littles can put something in a box. Teach them while they are young; have your expectations. Actually, little children LOVE to help with a dustpan and brush. While it might seem like a hindrance in that moment, it will help you a million times more as it becomes their habit as they grow up.

Pens, Felt Tips, and Pencil Crayons

Why are you keeping pens that have run out? Do you have coloured pencils that don't have any nib left at all?

With your children, get all the pencil crayons out, throw the dud ones away, and sharpen the others. To make your life easier, you can get an electric pencil sharpener. When I was a teacher, either I got Year 5 and Year 6 children to help sharpen pencils at break time, or I got blisters by doing every single one in my classroom at once. Utilise those pencil cases that are empty; either put like with like, or make it a case that you can grab and go for mealtimes and travel.

Those felt tips that have run out are annoying. With your children, make little lines on paper, and bin the ones that are of no use. Some colours are used more than others—maybe replace those?

Paint

If the idea of paints fills you with dread, I have some tactics to help them be creative and your life easier. I once looked after wild, 3-year-old identical twins. They were awesome but a handful. So, when they painted, I let them do it in the bath. Then once the painting was done, we just put the artwork to dry and ran the bath. Make sure the paint is water-based—you don't want to dye your bath a rainbow colour. But they could print their feet and hands and cheeks if they wanted. Then they had a lovely warm bath. It was all contained. The house was clean, they were clean, and we had wonderful artwork to boot.

Another way to make sure they can paint to their hearts content, without painting your walls and floor, is by using water colours. I actually really love doing it myself; it is so therapeutic. Even really little children can get involved. Now, I know what you're thinking—little children mix the colours. Yes, yes, they do, but it is okay. Things happen. Have a water cup and a kitchen towel close by, and model how to do it. They copy you. Tell them what you're doing and why you're doing it; encourage them and verbally praise them when they wash and dab their brush. What if they don't? Then have a baby wipe handy. Dry the palette with the kitchen roll, and clean with the baby wipe. It's quick, it's easy, and it's fun.

Paintbrushes, especially if cheap, can tarnish pretty quickly. Do soak them in water, and then sort them out while the kettle is boiling for your brew, later in the day, or get rid of them. The cheap ones that are ruined and no longer work are wasting space in your house. Try not to get super cheap ones; ones with wooden handles can be recycled. I am really starting to think of the environment in all that I do, including all things child related. Again, if we do the hard work now, our children will benefit in later life, but more on that in the "Environment" chapter, Chapter Seven.

Playdough

Don't get this in the carpet—easier said than done, hey. We don't want it on their shoes and trampled through the house. Having a cloth under their chair can help this. Before they go and play something else, checking if they have any playdough on their clothes or feet can help.

Children also like to squish different colours here too. It all ends up in a vaguely brown/grey mess, which is totally unappealing. Playdough that isn't in an airtight container goes hard and is useless. Oh, and if the playdough is inside that mechanism in the ice cream maker or hair thing, then it is rendered useless. It is not only up to you to clear that. After every playdough session, work as a team to tidy it all up. If it is hard or a weird grey colour, bin it. You don't have to spend lots of money on playdough; there are many recipes online. They can choose the colours and even the scents, and then it can be kept in one of those takeaway containers and binned after not too long. I keep all the playdough pots to reuse as well. Waste not, want not. Don't keep broken ones, and don't keep ones you don't wish to use. Don't keep them for the sake of keeping them. My dad is one of those that keeps everything, and I mean everything. If he sees something that might be useful in five years' time ON THE STREET, he will pick it up, bring it home, and wash it. I bet more than half of the things he has kept will never be useful.

Remember, I said that the role-play corner with the little kitchen is really useful to help them develop. Well, this is the time to combine two things; technically, three. Playdough is amazing for building up fine motor skills, by using the playdough implements to cut and mould. Then, adding it into role play, popping it in the oven or in a pan really brings their learning to life.

They do need training in not leaving playdough in there. Consequences are how they learn. If they do it once and the playdough needs to be binned, then fine. But then don't make a new batch, and definitely don't buy a new batch for a little while. We all learn from mistakes. I just want you guys to learn from my mistakes in order to help your life be a little easier.

Sticky Stuff

Glue is so sticky, isn't it! I now collect the *Metro* or the *Evening Standard* from tube stops; not only to attempt the crosswords and sudoku, but to put under any artwork we do, paint or glue. It turns out, in my teacher life, I was a thief. I used to go to get free newspapers from the Co-op near my house in Manchester, to take to school to protect the tables. The THIRD time I popped into the convenience store at some ungodly hour, before the sun had even risen, I noticed that those free newspapers I had been taking, actually had a price tag on them. I was mortified and actually never stepped foot in that shop ever again. So, if you go for free newspapers, do check that they are indeed free! This is the perfect time for that embarrassed emoji face. If I am ever back there, I promise I will buy lots and lots of newspapers from them, AND donate the £1 I must have accidentally stolen from them. See, you are learning from my mistakes.

Glue is sticky. I know we established that in the last paragraph, but because of that, keep the artwork separated until it dries. In the classroom, we used to put washing lines up, and peg the artwork up. It acts as a display, keeps them up and out the way, and lets them dry. Obviously, if they are swamped in glue, that won't work.

A note on glue sticks: the cheap ones don't work. They dry out even when the lid is on, and for the good brands, they definitely need their lids on tight. It is best to bulk buy these items. Glue sticks are so useful for pretty much everything, but I also know that the school sends papers that they haven't managed to stick in books, or they did and they have somehow fallen out, probably because the glue they used was the cheap stuff. I was a teacher, remember?

And blue tac! It is always useful to have blue tac as you can display your pictures on the window—not on your walls, as that will bring the paint or wallpaper off. Windows, and perhaps cupboard doors that are not varnished, are okay. Just use a cleaning wipe after you've taken it down, and it should get rid of that grease mark that it leaves. When I was a teacher, you were assigned a certain amount of non-branded cheap tac. In one of my reception classes, displays kept mysteriously falling down. It came to my attention that it wasn't because the blue tac was so tacky (or not, as the case may be); it was because my children had decided they loved it so much, they would collect it and take it home! Staples on those boards were murder though. Trying to pry those pesky devils out was hard work at end of term.

Sticky tape is also sticky, but it is hard to find the end! There are many little devices with self-cutters that hold your tape ready to be used, but these can be dangerous for little hands. As with scissors, these should be used with an adult nearby. As they get older, they become more competent and are capable of doing this safely. If your children are really young, cut several strips and have them ready for them to pick, and before you pop your sticky tape away, just fold over the edge to stick it to itself so that the next time you come to it, you can easily snip that piece off and get on with crafting.

I keep all glue-related products in the same-labelled drawer or box. Keep like with like, and you'll always know where it is. Keep them out of reach of young children, especially glue guns. That always should be an adult-led activity.

Craft

I use takeaway plastic containers for all those pesky tiny pieces that children love, because they are stackable and see through. Your child can see what they want, so they can just open the tub they want. Inevitably, they will want to open all the containers, but if all the pieces were in the same bag, that bag would probably be tipped out on the floor, and then we would be standing on it for weeks to come.

If their options are neatly separated, it gives them more chance to be creative than if they have to try to find something that they think is in the bottom of the bag but can't find.

Keeping washed recyclable items is a great way to have a craft activity that costs you hardly any money. Toilet rolls, along with egg boxes, can be used for all sorts of things—give it a google. I make a bouquet of flowers with the children, out of eggs boxes, every Mother's Day. Keep it for a week, take a photo, and recycle. You don't need to collect dust along with bits of sellotaped cardboard. Declutter, organise, and live an easier life. Check out Chapter Seven, on the environment and recycling, junk modelling, and emotional or sentimental items.

Displaying Artwork

Kids make a lot of stuff, don't they? So, once you've taken it down from your washing line display, take a photograph of it. That way, you have it forever. Ask them to choose some but not all. Put the ones that they no longer need to keep, in the recycling. Get them into this habit. We can't keep everything. "We love all your work, but your best is what we keep in a physical copy." I bought an amazing frame that had a spring in it. You could pop them in and store lots of pages of artwork without having millions out. That meant their precious ones were kept safe. We also found another company where you send off the artwork and they make it into a book, but you could just as easily make one yourself. I make Learning Journeys for the children I work with; I love using Freeprints, which is an app where you get to print off 40 photos for free each month, and you only need to pay for the postage and packaging.

Gone are those days where you took the camera film to the supermarket and waited three weeks for them to process it, only to find out half of them were blurry. Oh, those were the days, weren't they! Or you can get an Instax camera, which is an updated version of the Polaroid, and I am pretty sure you do not have to shake the photo so that it doesn't develop blurry. Freeprints also has a book app, so you could make a book if you wanted; because, after all, "there is more to books than reading." Someone great wrote a book on that—don't know who it was. Oh yes, it was me! But the best thing about taking a photo of their artwork is that you don't actually have to print it off. It will pop up in your memories for years to come; or alternatively, for one child I looked after, we set up an email address and sent them off so that when she is older, she can have a giggle at all the photos she made us take of a feather stuck to coloured card. Just saying!

Then do a digital declutter, because you don't need 32 photographs of the same moment.

Musical Instruments

It's an important part of their development. Musical instruments help with maths and PE. How? They help with rhythm, which is pattern. They also help with fine motor skills, as well as with gross motor skills. Banging, shaking, scraping—all will in turn help your child with their physical development. So it is important that they have access to them. Some of these instruments will need batteries, so remember, as in the technology section, to make sure they work. If they are broken, you can take them to a recycling place. There was one near our local park, so when we had a few items, we just took them along—there was no need for a special trip. If they are salvageable, take them to a charity shop, especially if the musical toy in question is now too young for them.

Santa once bought G2 and G5 microphones that connected via Bluetooth so that you could play music from them. It was very kind of Santa. Take some paracetamol and settle down for the ride! But in all of this, have times when musical instruments are not available. Quiet time is just as important as noisy time. These items are ones that I would say to keep up high; of course, if they ask for them, bring them down. But set some time in the day where they go away again.

Calm and quiet time is just as important for their development as the other times, so to make your life easier, set a schedule. In that nanny role, I was 24/4, so I really do know what it's like. And you're going to say that I went home after four days—yes, I did, but I was also a travel nanny and proxy parent, who would go weeks without going home. What I am trying to say is that parents and nannies deserve a section of the day where it's not too noisy. So, you don't need my permission, but I am giving you permission. You are not a bad parent if you need some time where you can hear yourself think. So put that kettle on (put those paintbrushes away that you soaked earlier), and read a book while your child looks at books too. (They copy what you do, so show them that you enjoy reading too.)

ACTION

Which is the most unorganised?

Allocate these areas, from 1 being most and 6 being least.

- Felt tip pens and pencil crayons
- Paint
- Playdough
- Sticky stuff
- Craft
- Displaying artwork

Don't try and do everything at once. This is a marathon, not a sprint. Do little by little to make it achievable.

Oh, and always take before and after photos, and post on Instagram @more_to_organising #moretoorganising, or on the Facebook page, More to Books.

Competition time – How many felt tips and pencil crayons are in the bin? Send in a picture.

For bonuses go to ...

Notes

Notes

Notes

Chapter 5

Physical Development – Health and Self-Care

5

Physical development isn't just about exercise and fine or gross motor skills. Children should learn how to take care of themselves and be aware of what makes them healthy. This will set them up to be great adults; but before then, it will help you as they will become more independent, and then you won't need to help them all the time. But they also need to be more independent to succeed at school: changing for PE or swimming lessons, putting their own coat and shoes on for playtime, or changing into those amazing dress-up costumes to role play with their friends.

By organising their wardrobe and chest of drawers in a manner that helps them be more autonomous, and making sure the kitchen cupboards are decluttered and coordinated (by colour, wink), as well as keeping the bathroom free of dangerous substances, and having all the things for their self-care needs reachable and easy to use, they will be empowered to look after themselves.

It takes training. As with potty training, you are their mentor, their cheerleader, and the one to help when things don't go quite right. You can do this, and so can they!

Kitchen

Let us go around the kitchen and work out what the children can help with. As a nanny, I do "Baking Thursdays." I have done it in many nanny roles. The day before, I encourage them to go through recipe books and find something they would like to make. One of my children was a teenager doing her Duke of Edinburgh award, and a task was to make 25 recipes from scratch. While I did support her, I was more an overseer than the chef—showing where things are kept in the kitchen, where to get the ingredients from, and where the bowls and spoons and weighing scales are. If she can know this, it saves her time. I am an advocate of helping children, not just the teenagers, to become confident at making some meals from scratch. One of my children loved spaghetti carbonara so much that we experimented with different recipes and different ways, until it was something she could easily make with hardly any input from me. Obviously, I made sure all the ingredients were available, but actually giving her the confidence to switch up ingredients and put more of the things she liked, to make it to her tastes, are all skills she will need in later life. Not to mention perfecting chocolate chip cookies to wow friends in the future.

When I was at university, within the first month, I had gotten the dreaded fresher's flu and was held up in my bedroom really quite sick. The first day, I felt well enough to venture to the kitchen for some plain toast. Someone, who has turned into an absolutely wonderful friend (who can now cook delicious meals and curries), asked me to check if his burgers (of which he had squeezed the meat out of sausages and flattened into patties) were okay. I went back to bed after that. I clearly wasn't over my fresher's flu. But what I do feel from that moment, and not just about that friend, is that many teenagers end up at university not knowing how to cook at all. Have them involved in cooking from an early age. The more they do it, the easier it becomes, and the more independent they become along the way, helps you.

Getting a stool for a child can make them more independent to reach things that are up high. To be fair, I need one too! In my new nanny house, I am constantly having to stand on a stool to reach the higher shelves. In one house, the microwave was up high, so I would still advocate a nearby adult in that instance; but for other things, older children who are just not tall enough can be given more freedom, and it is safer than a chair. There are many companies that make boxes, for want of a better word, so that your little ones can help at the kitchen surface. Again, these need to be used with an adult. One child had happily stood on the box but tried to reach sideways for something. There are some that are heavy enough to withstand that, but an adult close by is imperative.

Tupperware

Tupperware is so useful for children. It is for batch cooking, leftovers, snacks, and even craft items. One of my nanny families wrote a reference for My Nanny Circle, which was published in the magazine for all the awardees. They said lots of lovely things, but one was that all their Tupperware had the correct lids. In my new nanny family, I had just organised their Tupperware drawer, and the dad couldn't believe how much space there was in there now. It was just because I put the rectangle Tupperware in each other, the circles in the circles, and the squares in the squares. It is all still there; it's just organised to put like with like, to utilise the space more effectively.

Visibility and Colour Coordination

So, I did get on the bandwagon of buying see-through containers in which to put my cupboard essentials. Check them out on Instagram @more_to_organising. Mine are plastic, which is good if you have children, but there are glass ones available if you would prefer to be more environmentally friendly. What is really good about having see-through containers is that when I am running low on something, it is really clear what I should put on my shopping list. In fact, even the children could help you with that. They are such visual creatures. When you do come in from doing the shopping, pour the little bit of rice in a cup, fill up the container, and put the little bit of rice on top, so you are using the older food first. It makes it really easy when you are cooking, as you can just pour out what you need. It has made me notice that I really don't eat red lentils enough! I don't actually label these containers, so you have the freedom to switch it up. One time it's red lentils, and the next time, you can put quinoa in, with the exception of self-rising flour and plain flour—it would be annoying to get those mixed up.

Your cupboards should be organised with your child in mind. What makes sense? What things do they need to be able to reach? What things do you not want them to be able to reach? While we are at it, what things do you not want to be able to reach all the time? Life is about balance. Keep things you want and need, in reach and visible, but those treats? Out of sight, out of mind. But they are there for when you want them.

Let's play a fun game. Your children can do this with you. Pull out all your tins. You could make a bar chart with them to see what you've got the most of. This also helps with that shopping list of yours. They can help you sort them into colours, or by item. Perhaps sort them with the things you use the most and the things you use the least. Put the ones you don't use very often on the highest shelves, and keep the ones handy that you love to use all the time. I like to use cupboard steps (go check them out on Instagram @more_to_organising) so that I can easily see what is there. If you don't want to use plastic, there are more and more wooden designs coming out. Before you put them back in your cupboard, get your children to check the dates on all your tins. See, they are learning maths, dates, years, months, and out-of-dates.

I have done this activity a few times. My dad is the current champion of having the oldest tin in his cupboard, at 1998, which means he moved house with it and still didn't eat it. Don't worry, I have gotten rid of it for him now. But it is always helpful to go through your cupboards every once in a while. When I worked at Marks and Spencer's Food, I was on the late shift, and I was the third date checker in the fridges. So, two people had checked before me, and I still found things that were going off that day. Take a picture of your oldest can and post it to me on Instagram @more_to_instagram, with the hashtag, #moretoorganising. Let's see if you can find an older one than 1998. My nanny friend once told me about a herb in her grandma's cupboard that was dated 2004. Close but no cigar.

Freezer

Batch cooking is your friend. It saves so much time. My favourite thing to make is a bolognaise (or a meat free one), and I make SO MUCH as it is versatile. With pasta, I put it in a lasagne, or pop mash or sweet potato mash on top for a cottage pie, or add some kidney beans and have with rice. Some people put it in tacos; my dad likes it in a jacket potato. I even have it on buttery toast. One batch and you've made a potential of 4 different kinds of meals. I tend to have a food plan, so I know what to pull out and when. I have seen memes about having to figure out what to make for tea every night. I am northern—British and northern. Dinner is at lunch time—school dinner, dinner ladies, Sunday dinner, Christmas dinner—it all happens in the middle of the day; let us not argue about it. Just accept that we say different things. Well, I have never understood this.

Being a nanny whose actual job is to make three meals a day, I coordinate (not by colour this time) different carbohydrate options and protein options. I saw an American nanny doing Meat-free Mondays and Try-it Tuesdays, on The Nanny Collaborative, which is a Facebook forum where nannies support each other and collaborate (it was in the name). I adopted it into my repertoire and also made it super easy, as sometimes I wouldn't know what would be in the nanny fridge from the weekend, but I could usually do a pesto pasta or some kind of jacket potato with beans or cheese. So, on Tuesdays, I'd always do chicken (with a new vegetable or food item); on Wednesdays, I'd do fish; and on Thursdays, I'd do red meat. Friday is usually pizza or burgers or takeaway with their parents. I actually have a four-week plan of different ideas. The thing with plans is that it has to make your life easier, and definitely be a guideline rather than be set in stone. While it does take a little time to plan, once that is done, it's actually much easier in the weeks after. And because you've batch cooked that bolognaise, you don't have to cook from scratch for about four weeks on Thursdays. Just pull it out of the freezer, defrost it, reheat it, and add the carb and the cheese—I love cheese!

Some days, you have swimming or club or this or that. Plan something super easy that day. Take any guilt away. On Thursday, their dinner was packed full of vegetables and nutrients. Some days, I do a "make-your-own," where I provide the ingredients and they put it together themselves. It's relatively easy for me, and they feel so autonomous. We have done pizzas (buy the pizza dough ready-made, or batch make and roll out and freeze until the day you want them), wraps, sandwiches, tacos, etc. They all involve some form of bread, but what I mean is, you've given them an array of vegetables, and they've had fun. You don't have to do something fancy. In fact, I have qualifications in weaning and children's nutrition. As long as you're hitting the basics, pat yourself on the back. Life with little children is like spinning a thousand plates—make the meal plates not ones you have to worry about.

Recipe books are your friend, as is the Good Food website. When cooking with children, I always write "easy" with the meal we want to make. The less steps, the better, if they are just starting to learn how to cook. But Annabel Karmel, Rebecca Wilson of *What Mummy Makes*, and Ella's kitchen, all have tried and tested ideas, packed full of those vegetables they need, and they tell you if you can freeze them, so it's easy to pick different things. They say it takes a child 18 times to really know if they like a new food. Put it on their plate. Encourage them to touch it. Present it in different ways, such as making carrots or cucumbers in ribbons rather than sticks. Don't force them to eat it, but don't give up presenting the new food as an option; just make sure you also offer something they definitely will eat.

Putting options in the middle of the table, and letting the children choose how much to put on their plate, prevents overwhelm and gives them autonomy of what they want to eat. When I was a child, my mum made me sit at the table until everything on my plate was finished. Much to the annoyance of my mum, a teacher had come to school and told us how awful chips were, and I was probably the only child that it stuck with. This was back in the days when we all had deep fryers in the kitchen, so they were slithered in oil. Well, I sat there for a very long time and finally did finish my cold chips. I don't know if you've ever had cold, deep-fried chips, but the fat stuck to the top of my mouth, solidifying any thoughts I had of liking chips. So, I don't eat chips! I will have the occasional French fry from McDonald's though; you know, it's all about balance.

Anyway, if your child is still struggling with the vegetable side of things, try not to show how much you're worried in front of them, and definitely don't talk about what they won't eat. In saying that, I hate mushrooms. What do you hate? What is your reason? I don't like mushrooms because they are slimy and remind me of snails, which I have also tried on French Day from a can when I was 10; and no, I don't like them either. If you don't like something for a valid reason yourself, your child doesn't have to like everything. Just thank them for trying it and say that they can try them again another day, maybe in a different way. Mushrooms are way less offensive on a pizza as they are usually not as slimy. Also, I've heard people cook them nicely in garlic or something. Maybe I will try them again. Obviously, having an intolerance or an allergy is totally different to just dislike.

Setting the Table

Children as young as three can help you set the table. If it is an expectation, they will support you. It is all about working as a team with the children. As a nanny, I always say, "I will do this; can you please do that?" You are not their slave; there are things that they are capable of helping you do, and this means there is less for you to do. Have the cups, plates, and cutlery in cupboards and drawers that they can reach.

Eating with your children might be tricky timing-wise, but I always tried to sit down with the children; even if I wasn't eating, I would have a small portion. Children copy you. Eating the same things as them, makes them more likely to eat what is on their plate. One of my nanny children was struggling with eating, but yet she would eat things off my plate. What was hers was hers, and what was mine was also hers! So, I would joke that the things on my plate were mine and she couldn't have any, so she would cheekily "steal" the vegetables off my plate and eat them for herself. I did it in a loving, joking way, where there were lots of giggles, and she ate!

Clearing Away

If everyone puts their own things in the dishwasher, from a young age, it becomes a habit that they won't even have to think about. Model scraping the food into the food bin, rinsing the plate or bowl, and popping it into the dishwasher. A note on the dishwasher, if they put it in wrong, praise them for putting it in when they are little. Negative feedback all of the time is as horrible for children as it is for adults. As they get older, praise them when they have placed it in correctly. The idea of this is to reduce your effort in clearing the table; and yes, it will be a little bit of admin to tweak the plates but a lifetime of not having to scrape and rinse—eventually, they will get there.

Oh, and not my trick, but one of the mum's that I worked alongside put straws to baby bottles, with the hole over the vertical prong in the dishwasher—you know, the ones that help support the plates to stand up—so that they didn't end up falling to the bottom of the dishwasher, and I also think they got cleaned more effectively as they were upright instead of horizontal. Bottles with straws should be taken apart and washed; there have been cases where mould has built up in the lid. If you only ever put water in them, they are less likely to do that, but they still need a good clean.

Keep a hand-held hoover by the dining/kitchen table. Children actually love hoovering and sweeping. The hoover is more effective than the dustpan and brush. But getting them involved from an early age, and praising them verbally for trying, even if they make a bit more of a mess while they are practising, will mean they become children and adults who do it as a second nature. With older siblings, I ask one to wipe the table, and one to hoover the floor, and I let them argue amongst themselves who does what! They always wanted to wipe the table. There has to be an order to it; it's no good them hoovering the floor and then wiping the table, as bits from the table inevitably end up on the floor.

Any cutlery that was not used can go back in the drawer, and you can get the children to put away the condiments. I am not saying that you sit back and do nothing; you're a team. You have cooked it (unless it's on one of the days you've cooked together), but I usually washed up the pans while all that was going on.

Under the Sink

Dishwasher tablets look like sweeties in wrappers. Put a lock on that door or move those items somewhere unreachable to children but within reach for you. What makes sense? You've just lugged a huge basket of laundry down, there is a hungry baby, and you need a brew (I always need a brew). By arranging your kitchen so that things are in the right place, as with the cups above the kettle in the introduction, you save time in the long run. The great thing about putting the dishwasher tablets in a cupboard above the washing machine, rather than below, is that you can take the child-lock lid off; so when you are popping one in, it's just a case of reaching. I don't even think I can undo those child-lock lids easily; I end up taking the whole plastic lid off. Also, the bags or boxes don't even have child-lock lids, and they are cheaper. If you have to put them under the sink, then please do use the child-lock lid ones. (How many times can you write child-lock lid in a paragraph?)

So how many times have you confused the dishwasher tablets for the washing machine tablets? I have picked them out and then with a puzzled look, gone to check the package before. With different brands, the tablets look different. If you are keeping these tablets in the same cupboard, keep them at opposite ends of the cupboard (for those who have washing machines and dishwashers in the same vicinity). It is much easier when you have a laundry room, as you never have to get confused. To make your life easier, always keep these items topped up. The dishwasher and washing machines never seem to be off in a house with children. I used to joke that I was ordered around by appliances when I worked full time. The oven would beep and then the washing machine would sing; the microwave would ping and then the washing machine would chime. As long as it wasn't the smoke alarm...I know what it's like. During lockdown, the dad was on a very important video call in the kitchen/dining room/living room, and I was trying to quietly make lunch while the children were finishing their Zoom school lessons, and there was a loud alarm sounding, so I quickly jumped onto a stool to try and turn the smoke alarm off, only to realise that the baby had set the oven timer hours earlier.

ACTION

Commit to working as a team and as a family.
Which is the most unorganised?

Allocate these areas, from 1 being most and 3 being least.

- Colour coordinate and check dates of tins.
- Freezer
- Under the sink

Don't try and do everything at once. This is a marathon, not a sprint. Do little by little to make it achievable.

Oh, and always take before and after photos, and post on Instagram @more_to_organising #moretoorganising, or on the Facebook page, More to Books.

Competition time – What is the oldest tin in your cupboard? Send in a picture.

Bathroom

When your child is poorly, this is definitely the moment when you need your medicines to be organised. There is nothing worse than finding an almost empty cough syrup that went off the year before, when you have big eyes that just need a cuddle in front of you. It's dark, and you're tired. Obviously—well, I say this is obvious, but I am about to tell you a story of my own childhood rebellion—keep medicines out of reach of children.

When I was under 7, because we still lived in our old house, I had been playing in the woods across the road from the house, and I must have decided that I was feeling a little ill and had gone into my parents' room to have the Calpol—you know, the delicious strawberry one? Well, first of all, I could reach it! Second, I must have been a smart kid because the child-lock lid was no barrier to me back then, and I had the appropriate 5ml by using the little plastic spoon (which can go in the dishwasher btw). I think I would have gotten away with it if I hadn't trodden dog poo all the way up the stairs and into my parents' bedroom! I think I tried to blame it on Drop Dead Fred as he was my invisible friend at the time—not very creative back then, not even being able to think of my own invisible friend; also, I have watched that film as an adult, and it is really inappropriate for under 7s, just saying, although all that stuff just went over my head.

So, keep it somewhere they can't reach and/or they don't know where it is. If they need medicine, they should have an adult with them.

Check the dates on those bad boys, and keep a stock of all things useful. Let's play the same game as with the tins in your kitchen cupboard. Clear out anything that is past its use, by date. Get rid of anything that has been open too long or doesn't even have enough for one dose. Wipe them down with a Dettol wipe to take the stickiness off. Recycle the cardboard boxes; you don't want to have to undo a box AND open a child-lock lid when you have a crying child.

Keep this topped up with plasters; did you know these go off too? I think it is maybe something to do with the glue. Being a runner, in my own medicine cupboard, I used to have many blister plasters ready for after a long training run, but then I found out about twin-skin socks and haven't had any blisters since. That's just a free takeaway for any runners reading. Oh, and while we are in the medicine cupboard, Body Glide helps with chafing when doing marathons; also have Imodium for runners' trots, and never use ibuprofen, because it thins the blood. Vaseline is great for your eyebrows on a hot day; I found that out the hard way while training for my first marathon in Cape Town, and having stinging eyes from all the sun cream running in. In 2018, the London Marathon was the hottest one on record, so me training in Tuscany and Cape Town really helped. But back to the children...

Being a teacher, nursery nurse, and a nanny, I have always had paediatric first aid training. There are some things you really need to keep in your house just in case. I hope you never have to use them, but make sure you have a first aid kit and a burns kit. During the first lockdown, I was so rushed off my feet from being the nanny, housekeeper, laundrette, chef, home-school teacher, IT support, and nurse—all while trying to be the emotional support for the parents as well as the children—I ended up having silly accidents and burning my arms a few times within a fortnight. I had the oven mitts on, but I had a short-sleeved t-shirt on, and the corner of the hot metal oven tray burnt my forearm. I still have the scars. Accidents happen. Looking back, I was overwhelmed and tired, so that is another reason why organising, delegating, and prioritising would have kept me from burning myself. Luckily, I knew what to do. I hope that you or your children never get hurt badly, but having these things can help you deal with accidents quicker whenever they do happen. I would advocate that every parent do at least one first aid course. I can't actually believe it is not mandatory. Even people without children, should have basic first aid drilled into them.

Teething gel for babies needs to be handy at night in the dark. Have plenty of those little plastic syringes. I love that these are a thing. When I was little, and I progressed from the nice tasting medicines to the horrible ones, I would move my mouth at the last second, so the gunky brown liquid would end up on my pyjamas. The mark would never seem to ever actually disappear, no matter how many times it had been through the wash (maybe stain removers have just gotten better too), but the syringes mean you can suck up the right amount of medicine into them that you need for the child, and it creates a lot less mess, I find.

I like to organise the bathroom shelves according to body parts. For the teeth, things need to be closest to the child, somewhere they can reach. Only keep one shampoo, conditioner, and body wash out (use a lavender scent to support them in sleeping—sleep training for the win), and keep spares put away. If your child loves to make potions, perhaps keep them out of reach if you don't want them all to be used up in one go.

I keep medicine up the highest, but you can also keep up higher the things that you don't use all of the time. Or at least keep the things within reach that you need to use all the time. If you have items you have never opened and don't intend to use them, give to charity, or items that you have opened but don't use, give them to a friend or family member with a child (or use these ones for the potions). Some items, your child will just have outgrown. Do you have baby lotion and your baby has grown up? It will probably be no good for anything now. You don't need it in your house. Rinse it out and recycle.

So, I like to organise by face, hands, body, hair, nails/feet, and medicine, and from reachable to out of reach. Little scissors, tweezers, and nail clippers, again, should be out of reach of children. Tweezers are so useful for getting out splinters—how do children get so many? I hardly get any as an adult. This was actually not a splinter, but I stood on a doormat in socks once, and I had such incredible pain in my heel. I had a tiny black dot, which turned into a huge red mound. I had to go to a podiatrist, and she spent half an hour fishing around in my foot, saying it must have gone as she couldn't find it, only then to find the TINIEST piece of fibre buried in my skin. It was as if my foot had decided to keep it. So, I never stood on those things ever again, and I now see the importance of slippers. It was a painful and expensive mistake.

Another thing children seem to get all the time are hangnails. I had never even heard of these until a few years into nannying. I don't even know what we called them. I think it is just a piece of torn skin near the nail.

Bathroom toys—they love them, right? I quite like the foam numbers and letters, where they can learn in the bath as well as get clean. Floaty things such as ducks can end up with disgusting mould inside them. My advice on that would be to get your hot glue gun out and seal up that hole. Or just don't get them in the first place. That makes me a party pooper, doesn't it? My new nanny boy says "fun sponge" instead of party pooper; I quite like that phrase. Anyway, check if they have holes before you buy them. There was an amazing video about rubber ducks that ended up in the sea, for children to learn about the ocean, where a shipment of 28, 000 plastic ducks fell overboard in 1992, and these little plastic ducks ended up all over the world. Scientists started tracking where they ended up. Can't make it up, hey!

Get the children involved in taking the toys out of the bath. You are a team. Even little children can help. If you have siblings in the bath together, I usually like to make it into a competition. I have a song for it and everything. It just goes, "Tidy up time, tidy up time, toys away, toys away, who is the quickest? Who is the fastest? It is (name of child)," to the tune of Frere Jacques. I actually just switch their names up and the amount of time. I always go for rewarding rather than reprimanding, if possible. Sometimes I throw my name in there just to verbally praise myself, because I do tidy up a lot. I always thank them for helping, and I always remind them that we are a great team.

I spoke earlier about actually painting in the bath to make it easier to clean up afterwards. You can get paints for the bath. They take a little bit of elbow grease to wipe off, but they do provide children with a lot of fun. When organising your life to make it easier for yourself, use the bath paints as a reward. Don't have them out all the time. For one thing, if they are there all the time, they get bored with them, and you will just have a lot of toys out and more to tidy up. ROTATE, ROTATE, ROTATE. And only bring the bath paints out when you have plenty of time, because your children are going to help you wipe the bath clean. On busy days, where they have had a club and it's dinner in 5 minutes, and something else is happening, that's not the day for the bath paints. The same goes for bubbles, by the way. One day a week, for fun, I make the bath so ridiculously bubbly. And I do mean the children's bath and not my own, because sadly, my new apartment doesn't have a bath.

Bath time can sometimes be a stressful experience, but I actually have never felt that way. I actually love the time where I get to sit down and have absolutely nothing else to do, other than sit there and have a chat and help them do their hair. I don't wash children's hair every day. It is dependent on sports clubs and PE days. However, toddlers and babies do need their hair washed. There was a number of times the "little man in my life" rubbed his hands through his hair at teatime (that's dinner to Southerners—see, I accept that we have different words for it), leaving bolognaise in it. I spoke about the routine of bath, book, and bed, which the *Supernanny*, Jo Frost, talks about. The bath gives your baby and toddler clues that it's about to be bedtime, and it winds them down. Add in that lavender I just spoke about, and bedtime will just be a calm, relaxing, and enjoyable time. Set them up for it and it will be easier for you. Babies, toddlers, and children thrive on routine. While it is tricky at the beginning to build or change your routine, once it is established, it makes for an easier life.

ACTION

Which is the most unorganised?

Allocate these areas, from 1 being most and 3 being least.

- Bath toys
- Medicines
- Self-care, where it is reachable

Don't try and do everything at once. This is a marathon, not a sprint. Do little by little to make it achievable.

Oh, and always take before and after photos, and post on Instagram @more_to_organising #moretoorganising, or on the Facebook page, More to Books.

Competition time: What is the oldest medicine in your cupboard? Send a picture!

Wardrobe/Chest of Drawers

Let's go into the bedroom. To help your child become more independent, they need to be able to reach their clothes. Using the Marie Kondo method of folding and rolling, and the Home Edit way of colour coordinating, your child will know where to find their favourite top, and they won't need to pull everything out; also, they will know where to put it back. They should definitely be involved in putting items away too. If they know where their sports kit lives, they can pull it out and put it in the bag for the class. That way, you just have to check it rather than do everything yourself. If you have multiple children, that's a lot of work for one person. Get them involved. Also, if they only wear that jumper for a couple of hours, don't wash it every time. When I was a little girl, I am pretty sure I only had one school jumper, which was probably given to me by my brother, and if I got yoghurt on it on Monday, then I had yoghurt on my jumper for the rest of the week. Now, I am not saying to only have one jumper, but if it doesn't have yoghurt on it, they can wear it another day. My nanny children tend to take off their cardigans at school anyway. Some things do not need washing every day.

Siblings

Things that are too big, put these to the back of the drawer. They are going to fit in them soon but not yet. If you put them in the loft, you might miss the window of when they do fit into them. So, you want them around but not "in use" just yet. For siblings, I organise the clothes the eldest has grown out of, and put them in boxes labelled with the ages. On the younger sibling's birthday, I pull out that box, and it's fun for both of them to see what they like, what fits, and to have some memories to talk about. It is important to note that children have different personalities, and they might not like some of the items. Donate these.

I don't think clothes have to be for a boy or a girl. If a daughter has a t-shirt, and her brother can wear it when he grows into it, or vice versa, then reuse those items. When I was 12, I thought my brother was the coolest. I was just starting to wear clothes to express myself. He had grown out of his checked shirts. I decided my style was jeans, a vest top, and his shirts. I saved my £5 pocket money for 6 weeks, and much to the disgust of my mum, I bought those trainers with heels, because I always wanted to be taller than I was. I don't know where I got that style from, but I thought I was cool, and that's all that mattered.

Rotate

This is the hardest area to rotate. My advice would be to always buy items that are a tiny bit too big for them, so that they last longer. If you put summer clothes away for a baby, unless they have siblings or you plan to have more, you will not use those items again. If they have some emotional attachment, put them in a special labelled box— we will deal with those in Chapter Seven. But for all others, give away, sell, or donate. Don't clutter your house with things you will not use.

Any items that are stained, ripped, or bobbled, either fix them yourself or take them to be fixed, and if neither of those work, get rid of them. In saying that, I also like to use those items for messy play. But don't keep loads of them. You only need one top that doesn't matter if it gets "ruined." Keep it separate from their normal clothes so that they don't end up on a playdate in the messy top. Also keep their special clothes separate. The clothes that they can reach should be the clothes they can choose for anything.

Pyjamas can be rolled up together; keep the shorts and t-shirt pyjamas to one side of the drawer, and the long-legged, long-armed ones to the other side. The thing about children (not babies) is that they can monitor their own temperature. They can choose, so give them the options. In regard to underwear, I was taught by another nanny to roll them so that they end up tucking into each other. This is a brilliant tactic because you can tell if they are clean. Until I had met her, it hadn't occurred to me to roll them in that way. I also colour coordinate their socks and underwear.

Coats and Shoes

Some items might fit again next year, such as snow suits, winter coats, and pyjamas. Put them away and try them on again just before the season comes back in. Accessories such as scarves will last another season, all the seasons perhaps, but gloves and socks, probably not. And hats ... well, their brains get so big. When it is the change of a season, make sure items that categorically cannot be used in that season are no longer taking up space in your day-to-day areas. We will talk more about this in Chapter Six.

Some coats will fit them the next season. Buy them slightly bigger, and keep them if you have younger siblings, and use them. If you're not going to use them, don't let them take up space in your house. When going on car rides with a child in a car seat, they should not be wearing their puffy jackets. This can cause them more damage if they crash. Turn your car on to heat it up before you get into it, or take a blanket and put it over them after you've strapped them in. The seat belts are designed that way. It is okay if you didn't know, but now you do, so please find an alternative way to keep them warm in the car.

Shoes! Have you ever tried to put shoes on a toddler who doesn't want them on? If you are reading this book, I imagine you have. Have you ever tried to put shoes on a toddler who doesn't want them on, AND they are too small? Your life is worth more than that. Put those shoes away for a younger sibling, or GET THEM OUT OF YOUR HOUSE. They do not deserve space in your abode. I had one child that would only wear her purple plastic cat shoes. The tail was the strap, which went round the top of her foot and Velcroed to the top. As time went on, they didn't really fit properly, and the Velcro got so worn that it no longer actually stuck. But she LOVED them. Pick your battles. I let her wear them to the park, but I took her trainers or wellies in the bottom of the pram. If she wanted to climb that frame, or go on that swing or in that puddle, she most definitely could, but she had to switch to the other shoes. It was a safety issue. They didn't stay on her feet, so she would end up tripping.

The pull of the slide was more important to her than the pull of the cat shoes in that moment. We didn't need to argue or fight about it—not in the house and not at the park. Also, "out of sight, out of mind" works in that situation too. If you hide those particular shoes just before you go out, you *might* get out the door without the cat shoes at all, but toddlers are toddlers. They are strong willed; they have personalities and you know about them, thank goodness. We are just guides. Unfortunately, cat shoes on the playground equals a hospital trip, so being the adult, I do have to support her in that.

ACTION

Which is the most unorganised?

Allocate these areas, from 1 being most and 9 being least.

- Underwear, socks, tights
- Pyjamas
- Legs
- Tops
- Hanging items
- Uniforms
- Sports kits
- Coats
- Shoes

Don't try and do everything at once. This is a marathon, not a sprint. Do little by little to make it achievable.

Oh, and always take before and after photos, and post on Instagram @more_to_organising #moretoorganising, or on the Facebook page, More to Books.

Competition time – How many items are not for this season? Are you storing them for next year or donating? Show how many bags are being sent to charity.

How are your rolling skills? Show me your drawers.

Prams

Those trainers, shoes, dirty socks, used wet wipes from last week, a lone Weeto or cheerio, a bag with the crusts of a sandwich, a stone, a twig, some random piece of toy that they just had to bring with them to Amanda's Action Club—who needs a reminder to look in the bottom of the pram? You know the worst place for me? It is in the fold of the hood. On one pram, it didn't have a handy pocket, so I would stuff that wet wipe in there, and then when it rained and I finally opened that hood, it would rain all the discarded bits and bobs from the week. If possible, try and empty that pram every time you come in. It is hard, I know. They are hungry or crying, or there's a delivery, or you have three siblings all fighting over that one toy that they wouldn't care about if no one was playing with it at all.

Organising your pram, and organising your life, makes life easier. Give yourself a break. First of all, if any of the items in the pram belong to the elder siblings, give them the responsibility of their own things. I looked like a donkey when coming home from my first job. I would have the boy's sports kit, the girl's violin, a lacrosse stick, all the coats, and then when the toddler got out of the pram, it would flip over due to the weight. We caught on that the big kids should clear the pram before the little one clambers out.

On the pram is usually the nappy bag as well. You can get amazing nappy bags now, with inserts for different items. They can help you be way more organised, but sometimes, with so many pockets, it just means that there are more places for your keys to get lost!

Before I would go out, I'd always recheck the bag. As a nanny, it also meant the parents used the bag, so sometimes it would be used and not topped up when I wasn't at work. If you're the only one using the bag, hopefully, things might not be taken out. Although, in one family, the toddler knew that snacks were kept in there, and he was a little sneaky with that sometimes. So little hands can also mean that things deplete.

I always take a change of clothes for children, up to about the age of 5, and especially if we are on a day trip. I would rather be prepared than have a cold, whiney child. When potty training, I take three resealable plastic bags with a whole clean, dry outfit inside. This means you can pop the dirty, wet clothes in the bag and seal it up. That usually gets thrown in the bottom of the pram to be dealt with when I get home. There was one particularly horrendous experience for both of us involved, when the little man in my life, who features in my first book, *There's More to Books than Reading —How to Help Your Child Bring Stories to Life,* had done a number two in his underpants, and we just happened to be walking through a cemetery. I knew they had toilets there, so I decided it was best to sort it out ASAP before he sat back in the pram and squished it into his undies. You feel me. I know that you know exactly what I am talking about.

Well, being that it was a toilet in a cemetery, it was not your cushy baby-changing toilet, with spare wipes like you get in Purple Dragon or even Marks and Spencer. I did not want to lay him down. So, we attempted the stand-up change. Only, just as the underpants dropped to the floor, and the little man in my life moved his foot to step out of them, instead of out, he went IN! Honestly, it was the worse change I had ever done—worse than poo explosions all up their back. Don't worry, I had plenty of wipes, and he thought it was hilarious. But I did put him in the bath as soon as we got back, and I made sure his toenails got an extra clean. Please make your life easier by learning from my mistake, but do let me know your worst nappy changing story! That story would have gone much worse if I hadn't made sure I had spare wipes and clothes and a little bit of humility. At the time, these events are dreadful, but as time passes, they are pretty funny. I can't cycle past that cemetery without having a little giggle to myself about that day.

Pets

Ah, pets! I have had a nanny dog, and I literally called her my third nanny child. I did proxy parenting for that role, and the dog would sleep in my bed at those times. In fact, I travelled with this family, and the dog would come with us to Italy too. My bed in the nanny house was a beautiful oak four-poster, but it did mean that she could not climb it by herself. She would whine to get off because she had smelt a wild boar or something, and then come back and whine to be lifted back on. Obviously, I loved her just like a nanny child. HA HA.

When I had a dog as a child, I would always have random poo bags (unused) in pockets. I'd be at school and put my hand in my school coat and pull one out. They have these really handy things now that just attach to the lead, so random bags don't need to be in your pockets anymore. I have a lovely nanny friend who has the most gorgeous sausage dog, and she has all sorts of handy gadgets. When my last nanny family got a puppy, I gifted them with a bottle that doubles up as a bowl. It is so clever and makes life easier.

Have a cupboard just for the dog or pet. Keep things by the door for walks, if possible. That way, they are handy on the way out but also on the way back in—remember from before, when you have the pram, the hungry baby, and the arguing siblings, but now you also have a barking dog. I feel you.

ACTION

The good news is that you might not have a pram, a nappy bag, or a pet, so you can go and have a brew. (Or check the car, garage, or loft. There is always somewhere.)

Which is the most unorganised?

Allocate these areas, from 1 being most and 5 being least.

- Emptying the pram
- Cleaning the pram
- Emptying the nappy bag
- Restocking the nappy bag
- Sorting the pet cupboard

Don't try and do everything at once. This is a marathon, not a sprint. Do little by little to make it achievable.

Oh, and always take before and after photos, and post on Instagram @more_to_organising #moretoorganising, or on the Facebook page, More to Books.

Notes

Notes

Chapter 6

People and Communities

6

Seasons and Celebrations

Rotate, rotate, rotate. Put the Christmas books away when you put the Christmas decorations away. And the DVDs. Am I the only one who still has DVDs? I have just organised a very dusty bookshelf. By organising and decluttering, it means you can do a quick wipe of the shelf. If they are that dusty, they definitely don't need to be kept. I am not as vicious as Marie Kondo, who says we should only keep 30 books. I am a book lover. I wrote a book on books. I think children need way more than 30 (but perhaps they only need 30 in their immediate vicinity, and then you rotate the seasonal ones?).

While I do love books, as an adult, I actually am not very attached to keeping the physical copy of them. I read and then give to a friend or family member; that way, I can chat about it with them, and my stipulation is that they give it to someone they think will love it too. Why not encourage this in your children? When they have become too old for a book, they could give it to a family member or a friend who has younger siblings. Not special ones with fond memories. But they are not all special, and they do not all have fond memories; in actual fact, aren't there some books we hate—some books that you really hope the child won't choose! There was one book at bedtime that just had a lot of words, and it was later than it should have been in the routine world. I tried to paraphrase the paragraphs, but G3 wasn't having any of it. She knew exactly what the words were, and I had to go back and read it properly.

Halloween

I am writing this just after Halloween. The Halloween candy is still going strong. Out of sight, out of mind is what we are trying, although it is still quite close and they haven't forgotten. In other families, we have put it out of sight, and then sometimes it has been forgotten about totally, and some delicious sweets that are loved have gone out of date, or ones that we all absolutely hate have gone gungy and disgusting. Get rid of those now. Go through the candy and donate any of the sweets that they just won't eat, to someone that will. Maybe wrap it up for birthday presents or Christmas presents.

Pumpkin carving kits can be put away with all those decorations. Some won't last the test of time. Some are super tacky, no? Put the paper and cards in recycling. Anything that is broken, don't clutter your house with it. Label the box, and remember where you put it. I've been asked a number of times to buy more Halloween things, only to find them randomly spread out about the playroom, or hidden in a random cupboard. Save your money and save time by having a place for everything and everything in its place. If it helps, put a note in your phone for where you have put it, and set it for a couple of weeks before Halloween.

Unless you've bought Halloween costumes big enough to last two years, or you have younger siblings, it's time to donate those costumes. It's very rare that children want to be the same thing every year anyway. The accessories or capes and hats will still fit. So, box them up, label them, and keep them somewhere you will remember for next year. I keep talking about rotating. If you bring these items out at the right time, they will last longer. Wigs are the bane of my life. I never thought I'd say that phrase. The wigs that children get are usually pretty bad quality and end up smelling really bad. They need to be brushed and hung up. So, being the party pooper or "fun sponge," I would rather not have them at all; but hey, if you keep them nice, then they can provide a lot of fun.

Face paint is a little bit like the water colours from earlier. They get messy, but if you wipe them down, they'll be almost as good as new. Store away from little hands so that you don't end up with a mess just before going to nursery/school. Also, we like to put face paints on our arms so that it's not as difficult to scrub off and doesn't transfer to pillows, or jumpers as much when hugging. It can be a great time waster by letting them draw all over your arm, just saying. When I say "time waster," I mean that it supports their fine motor and creative skills!!!

Bonfire Night

You wouldn't think there would be much to say here, and I suppose there really isn't, but I had to share the anecdote about the sparklers because it's too good not to share. When I was a nanny in Italy, we had to be careful of vipers because we were in the countryside. Vipers are venomous snakes, and if they bite you on the leg, and you are far from the nearest hospital, you'd probably need your leg amputated; and if they got your neck, you'd probably die. Now, I have a huge fear of snakes, so I probably looked horrified at this information, to which the chef said, "What are you worried about?" And I answered, "Well, if I saw a venomous snake, I might faint; but also (pointing at the toddler and the little child), they have necks close to the ground!" Not me but the other nanny saw one on a dog walk, with the toddler asleep in the pram. I did see one slithering up the window in the courtyard, and my heart rate went up on my Apple watch.

So, what does this have to do with organising? It's a great question. On bonfire night and at New Years—or just on a random summer evening where we decided to have a fire pit, with powder that makes the flames go blue and green (oooooooh), and when the dad decides to show his party trick to the guests and spits alcohol in the fire and almost takes his eyebrows off—we also had sparklers. Putting a carrot on the end of the sparkler means the child can hold it more safely. There is always a risk with sparklers, and it should be done with extreme care. Explain the dangers to the ones that are old enough. With younger ones, hold the sparkler with them and let them guide your hand. Don't wear a fancy dress when using sparklers, as they are flammable. (Incidentally, don't ever let your child sleep in a fancy dress, for the same reason). Our sparklers were kept in the outside toilet.

One day, a viper had taken up residence in the outside toilet. Someone must have left the door open. The dad was lighting cardboard and throwing it in the outside toilet to try and scare the snake out. I reminded him that that was where all the sparklers were kept. Luckily, we didn't set fire to the house. But the snake didn't come out at that time. We left the door open overnight, and it did leave at some point. We called it the "snake toilet" after that, and it took us a few days before we would use it again, but when you're dripping wet from the pool, it's kind of the only option, so eventually we did use it again, warily.

So if you do keep sparklers somewhere, don't throw in bits of cardboard lit with flames, which is the takeaway from this section.

Birthdays

Wrapping paper, balloons, party favours, and candles—how many times have you rebought these things? I have worked with families that have wanted a different theme for each party. I have made hundreds of pastel coloured pom-pom puff ball things (and taken them down to store), and the next time they want a different colour. I am all for decorating and changing themes. I love that, but you don't need to keep the balloons that have the number 2 on, when you don't have the intention of having any more children.

When tidying up after a party, have three sections: keep, donate, and bin. Paper that hasn't been ripped to shreds can be reused, and cards can be displayed for a little while, but then why not pop them in the creative box for the children to reuse when making craft or cards for other children. Keep some that have emotional attachment, and store them with the other things in this category. I have cards from my gran and grandparents, which make me happy and emotional, but mainly happy. I love that I have that love from them, and I love that I have their handwriting, even now. And I think it's important to keep things like that. Some cards from other children don't need keeping. I do like to let the children have a "precious things" box. So, they can keep some things that are important to them. But the rest, reuse or get rid of them.

Duplicate toys, presents that you end up having more than one of, can be regifted or donated and sold. Just make a note of who gave it to you, so that you don't regift it back to that person.

Christmas

WOOOOOOOHOOOOOOOOOOOOOOOOOOOOOOOOOOOOOOOOOOOO OOOOOOOOOOOOOOOOOOOOOOO!

I LOVE CHRISTMAS. Can you tell?

Oh, I am so excited to share how to organise your Christmas decorations to make life easier for yourself. I love taking them down as much as I love putting them up, because I get so much joy from organising. Yes, Marie Kondo, I get joy from organising, just like you.

I am actually against tinsel. I find it hugely tacky, but I support your decision to use it. Not really; it shreds, so you have to hoover up a lot, and then the hoover gets unhappy. And it's not great for the environment—but hey, you do you. I do actually have one string of thin tinsel, and that does make me happy. I have strings of beads rather than tinsel. To store them, I wrap them around a cracker, which I also put in the tree for depth. Crackers are not very environmentally friendly, and the prizes are often plastic rubbish. You can check the back of the box to see if what is inside is useful. I quite like the pens and egg cups, or the screwdrivers that are so handy for opening the back of toys or those musical books. But put it somewhere and REMEMBER where it is.

Where do you keep your baubles? I keep my baubles and hanging decorations in Christmas coloured tins, and I put the tins under the tree so that they look like presents. I recycle all the packaging that the decorations come in, as I sometimes find that it's too easily breakable, and it actually takes up more space than it needs to, with the exception of my Disney baubles. Every year, I buy one more—well, I let myself buy one more, but sometimes it's four. I have undressed many trees for work. I have worked for a family where the parents were separated and I worked in both households, so I had double the trees to "undecorate." One of the families I worked for had special zip boxes that had dividers, so you could easily put the baubles away. In other families, we use tissue paper or kitchen roll. I also keep it all to reuse the next time they are put away. I like to be as sustainable as possible.

There is a lot of talk about whether to have a real tree or a fake one. Fake ones are very plastic... But I suppose if you are using it every year, then it is sort of sustainable as you're reusing it. I always get a real one, a 6-foot one. It's the smell—and the reason I like it so tall? It's because of the memory of going to my grandma and grandpa's house and looking up at their gorgeous tree. When I got older, I realised it wasn't actually that tall. It was because I was so small. But to get that same feeling, I like to have a very tall tree. My nanny friend gets a real tree every year too, but she buys one in a pot and puts it in her garden, so it grows and she brings it back in the year after. I don't have a garden, but that is a brilliant idea. There are now companies that deliver trees in a pot, and they take it away for you and bring the same tree back to you the next year. That would be really helpful for decluttering and organising.

I think what I love about having Christmas decorations up is the colour coordination and the twinkly lights. But then I love taking them down because of the feeling of making my space all neat and tidy again. When I was a teenager, I used to move my room around all the time. I think it meant I would find that jumper that had fallen behind the bed, and it kind of felt like I had a new room. One time, I made a corridor all the way around by using the wardrobe, bookcase, and chest of drawers, so I ended up with a tiny, square bedroom. I think it was just me trying to express myself. I am still someone who likes order and change. I did the same with my studio flat; I had my bed in every corner I could.

I think, with the Christmas tree, if I ever have children of my own, I might be a little like Monica in *Friends*, and have a side for me and a side for them; or I have joked that I'd have one for them and the main one for me. I just like things colour coordinated.

Even when my Christmas decorations are put away in see-through boxes, they look neat, and it brings me joy to look at them. I am itching to put them up. When I used to work in Cape Town for Christmas, we would leave around the 15th of December, so I always got my tree on the 15th of November to get my money's worth. I would undecorate it the day before. I actually had a party once, and my nanny friends and I had a few glasses of wine and undressed my tree. That was a lot of fun. I wanted to donate my tree to someone else that could use it over Christmas, but "he" was looking rather sad after a month, and no one wanted him. He is called "Bruce," by the way. I always call him Bruce. I will be on Bruce 8.0 this year. But he isn't a spruce. I always get a Nordmann fir because they are supposed to drop less needles, but also because I like how the branches go.

Anyway, no one wanted Bruce, so I left him in my studio flat over Christmas, and we actually went to Italy and the Maldives that year. We flew back and I suffered majorly with jet lag from the time difference and looking after the girls, whose body clocks were also confused, so their sleep schedule was a little shot. When I did go home, I dragged poor Brucey out of my flat and down the stairs. I pulled him round to the bins, in just a T-shirt and jeans, at some point in early January. I got back to the front door and realised I didn't have my keys! I rang the doorbells of a couple of my neighbours. One asked me how she would know if I actually lived there, and I said, "Well, if you let me in, I can show you my driver's licence, which is in my flat." Luckily, I had propped my actual flat door open to pull the tree out. I also said, "If you let me in, I can sweep up all the needles that have left a trail behind me."

So, I learnt from this, and not only did I take my key and wear a hoody the next year, I wrapped Brucey up in a fitted sheet, so I didn't have to spend an hour with the dustpan and brush on the communal stairs. I have a lift in my new building, and even though it is November, I saw a couple of needles in the lift. Someone got a tree already!

Easter

It is much the same as the advice from Halloween. Eat that chocolate before it goes off. You would think that would be obvious. I mean, chocolate would not last long in my house. I am sure I have bought someone an Easter egg, only to end up eating it and having to replace it before I met up with them. In one family, when organising a toy cupboard, I found a mottled Thornton's Easter egg.

Any cute craft related products can go away until next year. Supermarkets and craft shops sell little bunnies, chicks, and sheep. Unless you're putting them in small world, put them away. If they have lost an eye or a leg, get rid of them.

This brings me to Easter bonnets. If your child's school has a bonnet contest, take a picture of it, take the bits off, and reuse the hat if possible. Perhaps display it for a fortnight. I don't see the point of keeping it on display all year. If you want to keep it, put it in the labelled box and keep it for next year. Displaying it all year will make it dusty, and it will discolour.

Other Celebrations

While I have mainly worked for atheist or Christian families, as a teacher and a nanny, I use the calendar to help children learn about other celebrations, cultures, religions, customs, and foods. I think it is really important to get books about all different kinds of celebrations (Diwali, Valentine's Day, Burn's Night, St. David's, Shrove Tuesday AKA Pancake Day (have you ever had a pancake-only day, for breakfast, lunch, and dinner?), St Patricks Day, Mothering Sunday, St. George's Day, Queen's Jubilee, Eid al-Adha, Chinese New Year, Father's Day,

Remembrance Sunday, Hanukkah, etc.)

It opens the door for them to ask questions, and it means you can help them find the answers; you might not know the answer, and that is okay. To help your child become more independent and a wonderful adult, it is important to help them learn about the world and the communities and the people we share it with, with kindness and compassion. What they will find is similarities as well as differences. If you organise your craft activities, it gives a purpose to the activity as well as a learning option. If you organise your meal plan to try foods from different celebrations and cultures, it might open their taste buds and help them learn about food around the world. If you organise trips to see different cultures, it will open their world.

And from a decluttering and organisation point of view, an example from my nanny life, we have dragons, lanterns, and fortune cookies. Keep them out for a little while but then store them, label the box, and remember where you put it so you don't buy it all again. The fortune cookies should be eaten or given away before they go out of date.

While some things in our calendar have ended up as a marketing ploy for the card and gift companies, I like to make homemade cards (Design Technology coordinator for the win) and homemade gifts with the children. Photo frames are easy and fun to do and are useful. I like to encourage children to make little books about their parents. You can find printable ones online. I tend to use Twinkl.

Travel

Travel is another way to help them learn about other places, cultures, and foods. It helps with geography and history too. Organising so that it makes your life easier means everything is where you can find it. I keep my travel hairdryer and plugs in the same place. Passports, ESTAs, and now, I guess if you have one, a printed Covid pass too, I keep in a fireproof set of drawers, where I also keep other important documents like degree certificates and contracts. These need reorganising every now and again. Things end up where they are not supposed to be. Envelopes end up in there, which can be recycled.

Being a travel nanny, I have mentioned some of the places we have been as I talked about organising other things such as sparklers and the debacle of the Christmas tree. When I was 21, I was a nanny on a cruise ship, for a family who took fifty of their closest friends and family, and two nannies. I was one of them. I have mentioned them in my first book, as I blocked up the plug to the shower when leaving Germany, so that the children could float their new boat—which could have been a disaster! Thankfully, it didn't end up so. I took jigsaws, children's books, papers, and colouring pencils on that trip. The other nanny was so impressed that I had thought to do that. I planned on the fact that they might not have those things, and if they did, well, they had more. New items that they have not seen before are inviting.

On that trip, I went as far as Russia. I had been to Russia another time. I was flown out and put up in a five-star hotel, and I had my own driver for a half-hour interview for a job on a yacht based from Malta. I didn't take the job because I chose the travel job instead. But having prosecco at breakfast, while having a harp being played in the background, was quite the experience.

On my first trip with the travel nanny family, we went to an island in the Scilly Isles, then to Switzerland, and then to Italy. When packing for myself and the children, I had to organise clothes for British weather, clothes for snowy mountains, and then clothes for sunny swimming pool days. The trip was about three months. Luckily, we were flying private, so unlike other families I had worked for, the amount of luggage wasn't really a problem. However, the bag that would go to the Scilly Isles was on a helicopter, so I had to figure out separately what would be needed for Italy and Switzerland, for the bag that would stay on the plane, and what we would need for all destinations. I must say, I am really good at packing now.

When organising things that are not clothes, like in the cruise work trip, kids need entertainment. Having paper and pencils and reading books can mean that you can entertain on the plane or in the airport or at the table for meals. I never went anywhere without at least a pen, because napkins make great hangman or "nought and crosses" paper.

When organising medicines and toiletries, we tended to have a separate set of everything as we did travel so often. Sometimes I felt like I barely had my feet on the ground; we'd get back from Italy, and then 6 or 7 weeks later, we would head off to Ibiza or Mozambique. In the flight bag, we would have the toys and things, but also pyjamas and a spare change of clothes. I accidentally left the first aid bag at an airport in Africa, so we lost our first aid scissors that time. You live and learn.

Check the dates of your sun creams, after-sun creams, and medicines. You can get Calpol sachets, which I tend to take with me on day trips and not just travel trips, as they are already in the 5ml dosage.

When I am packing, I write a list of all the things we need, and tick them off over the couple of weeks before. I am always packed a week before the trip, so then I have that week to buy and top up the things that I haven't found in the house. The more you do it, the better you get at it. Layers for the children are important, and things that get missed sometimes, such as goggles, floats, and swim toys. It's okay saying that you can buy extra stuff. You can. It isn't the end of the world, but then you'll end up with 16 floats. Where are you going to keep them all?

I once went to Cape Town with only one pair of knickers, the ones I was wearing! I was on shift for 24/4 so didn't have time off to go shopping as I was working. I had to tell my boss so we could nip to a shop with the children, and I got a pack, only to realise I'd accidentally bought size 8, which definitely didn't fit. I just wore them until my day off, and then I went back to the Victoria and Albert Waterfront to get the correct size. They have Woolworths there. They are not like our old Woolworths; they are more like a Debenhams or something.

I want to tell you a funny anecdote about a trip over Christmas there. In Woolworths, while buying my correct-sized underwear, I also snapped up some wine for about 60 Rand, at the equivalent of £3. YES, PLEASE. I had a couple of nights off, and I figured if it's awful, it's only £3, and if it's nice, it's £3. Win-win. Plus, you can take the Northerner out of the North, but you can't take the North out of Northerner. This saying also works for the weather. I had a boss that was baffled that I used to run in the rain. If you don't run in the rain up north, you'll never run! Anyway, on Christmas Day, although I wasn't working, I was invited to each dinner with the family, and I asked if I could have the last glass out of the bottle I had. Their guest was like, "Why are you letting her drink this?" And the Dad said that I could have anything out of their wine cellar. Honestly, I didn't take anything from their wine cellar even after that. I love a bargain.

Donating and Charity

I have actually talked a lot about this already. At Christmas and birthdays, we do end up with multiples of things. A child I nannied loved Moana when it came out, and for her fifth birthday, EVERYBODY bought her Moana things. Great. We put them to one side and regifted.

Before a birthday or Christmas, get the children into the habit of putting some items aside that they have grown out of or just simply don't play with, to give to others that perhaps have less than them. I think it is so important that we look out for other people. People and communities in the EYFS are about being part of something. Schools have charitable fairs and raffles sometimes, so perhaps join in with that. Why not encourage your children to research about something that they really care about, and maybe go to a car boot or garage sale and give the money to a charity of their choice.

As in the kitchen section, I bet you have towels that have stains on them. I certainly do. I am not saying to change them for new ones for the sake of changing them. I still use my tea towels with stains on, but at some point, they do need switching out. The great news is that charities for animals, especially hedgehogs, take used towels in. Research it with your children.

With one family, there was a doorstop pickup, which asked for food and toiletries; get the children involved with collecting the items and sending them off. Most supermarkets have a place where you can donate food for charities, and your local churches might have a food drive as well, for people who need it. So, if you have food that you have extra packets of in your cupboard, which perhaps you're not going to eat—like my extra packet of red lentils that I bought, being over-zealous about my health and learning that I'm not as fond of it as I want to be—and when you go through your cupboards to check the dates, maybe see what items (that are in date) can be donated to a worthy cause. Helping your children do this now, will mean it is a habit, which means it will be second nature to them. They will become more grounded and hopefully more grateful, but also lovely adults.

ACTION

I actually think it only makes sense to organise these just after the celebration, but as you play with your children, collect items for that season or celebration, and pop them in a labelled box. Remember where you put it.

Post on Instagram @more_to_organising #moretoorganising, or on the Facebook page, More to Books.

Notes

Notes

Chapter 7

Environment

7

Fix

In one of my roles, the little girl had a lovely cardigan, which was by quite a nice children's designer, and one of the buttons had gone missing. These buttons were lovely but odd shaped pearlesque buttons. First, I contacted the seller to see if we could buy the exact button from them. They were really responsive and tried to be helpful, but unfortunately, the item in question was no longer being made, so they did not have any buttons to give, never mind sell. So, this sent me on a button quest around London. First, I tried all the little markets, but they didn't have any. Then I went to haberdasheries in department stores, which also did not come up trumps. The final place I went to, after asking other nannies where they went to buy buttons, was a lovely little place called MacCulloch and Wallis, near Oxford Circus if you want to know, and it is a colour-coordinated person's dream, by the way. Oooooh, so beautiful, and the height of organisation—I mean, you have to be with tiny buttons, no?

They were so helpful, and they got all their pearlesque buttons out for me but to no avail. Sadly, these buttons were super unique. So, they suggested that I choose a "statement" button and have the top button swapped out to the place where the button was missing. I chose a sparkly one for G7 to have as her top button. She loved it. How can this make your life easier? Don't go to all the button shops to find there are no buttons (no right buttons). Save time and get a statement button!

I have an amazing friend who can knit and sew, to whom I took items and she fixed them. In return, I plied her with wine and chocolates. I also have learnt to sew in recent years—being DT coordinator will do that to you. Having to teach children how to sew (I use wool, large plastic needles with big eyes, and paper with holes punched out to start their journey) means you become "okay" at doing it yourself. In fact, I went through a phase of sewing my own Christmas decorations, which I still put on my tree. I have an Osborne book of Christmas things to make and sew. But that meant I got quite handy at sewing in my nanny roles.

Sewing names on items became a huge job when I first started, but I can save you time on that as well. Mynametags.com has stickers for clothes, which can be ironed on, and ones for bottles and packed lunches, which are microwave and dishwasher safe. Having their items labelled means they can find them at school more easily, and it means you don't keep having to replace the hat, the scarf, the bottle, or the cardigan. Also, when I was a teacher, a parent would come and say that so and so had lost his jumper. I would ask if it had his name on it. No? But it's red and it's aged 5. Yup, so is the rest of the class. Actually, funnily enough, you know whose jumper it is from the smell. But if they've left it in the dinner hall, the jury's out.

My teenage nanny child was going to France for a school trip where they stayed over for the weekend, and the instructions were to label everything. I am one for following rules, so I even labelled her knickers, which she thought was hilarious, and all her friends thought I was really funny after that. I did just choose plain stickers with her name in black, and they were small. For children, on that website, they can choose the colour and a little picture; so if you have siblings, you can choose a different colour and a different picture. That way, they still have their name on, and it can be read by children of reading age; but also, your little ones who can't read yet, are capable of identifying their own items at nursery or preschool too.

If you can't sew, find a friend who can, or take items to a laundrette. One of my toddlers was given a beautiful little bag, which she insisted on taking to Caterpillar music. When she was running down the hill with it, through no fault of hers, the string snapped and the beads went flying all over the pavement. We picked them all up, and I put them inside the bag. Just before we went into the class, I dropped it off at the laundrette and, three days later, her bag was like brand new.

I was brought up in a world of fast fashion and, at university, we would go to Primark to buy an outfit just for that night. I don't do that anymore; I am definitely someone who wants to care for our planet. I now have a rule, being a declutterer/organiser and sort of minimalist, that I have one item in, one item out, or vice versa. So, if it can be fixed, I fix it. But if it can't, I replace it (if it's so important that it is an item I need, like running trainers). I still have more items than I wear all the time, and I have my favourites, but I don't want to buy anything more unless I need it. It is different for children; they keep growing.

Reuse – Toy Libraries/Libraries

Children like things that are new. Adults do too. And I don't mean brand new; I mean new to them. That's why it's so exciting to get a different car—because it's different. So, using a library for books means the books are more exciting because they are not there all the time. And they will not be there forever either. It is time limited. I have used toy libraries before as well. You do pay a little bit, but much less than buying it for yourself. I do keep them separate from their normal toys, which also means they are quite exciting. And it also saves your sanity when it's time to take them back; all the pieces are together.

Companies are starting to let you borrow items such as bags and clothes as well, like designer ones. This isn't helpful for your children necessarily, but it might make you feel great for the evening. Why not have a date night and book a babysitter? But they probably do have clothes for children if you have a wedding to go to in the near future. Or if you're a nanny reading this, let's go to the Nanny Ball in New York, with My Nanny Circle and with your borrowed frock. Incidentally, that is where I received the award for exemplary work in the nanny industry, in 2019.

Recycle

As I mentioned earlier, I was a teacher up north for 6 years before I moved to London. I was on a very low salary but somehow spent a lot of money on my wonderful children. The school's budget sometimes wouldn't stretch, and I wanted the activities and learning to be fun. But that also means that you wash every milk bottle to collect 60 to make a memory of elephants for a two-form entry class, or keep your egg boxes to make flowers, or any cardboard and plastic for junk modelling. Egg boxes and toilet rolls were actually banned in some of the schools I worked in, as they were worried about germs, but as a nanny, using their own toilet rolls and their own egg boxes, or indeed if it's for your own family, you don't have to think so hard about that.

We have talked about crackers. You can make them out of toilet rolls and tissue paper. Let the children choose what to put inside. Reduce the amount of plastic rubbish by popping in a sweet. They can write their own jokes and make party hats. They won't go bang, but they will help recycle and reuse items.

I also mentioned about recycling wrapping paper for other presents; if not to give to anyone else, at least for a pass the parcel. My dad used to do that every year with our Christmas paper, for the family party around New Years. When I was a teacher, we used to make our own wrapping paper with the children. It really helps with patterns. You could buy plain coloured paper and use stickers or stamps to decorate it for birthdays or Christmas. Recently, I found out that wrapping paper cannot be recycled, which is a little shocking. Brown paper can be recycled, and you can upcycle it to be decorated with stamps. I actually really like the look, but if you don't want that, use coloured paper and wrap accordingly, all the while teaching what goes next in a pattern.

We have already discussed reusing cards to make your own cards with the children. My dad used to cut up last year's Christmas cards to make gift tags.

Emotional Attachment – Clothes and Artwork

Children grow so fast, don't they? I always used to say to my children that I look after, that the word "can't" should not be used. If they tell me they can't do something, I encourage them to think of how we can go about it so it can happen, by trying, by doing something differently, or by asking for help. It is so important that they know they can ask for help. They don't have to do everything alone (and neither do you); but one day, I said to G3, "Stop growing up," and she said, "I can't." That is literally the only time I will allow that. It's true; she is going to grow. Her mum was quite attached to some lovely clothes that both the girls had worn, and they had fond memories of the times they had worn them. Although they no longer fit, we didn't want to donate them or give them away, so I researched a company where you sent a few items off, and they transformed them into a soft toy. They had lots of choices of what they could be, and we did just that.

There are lots of options on Etsy or other places that will make quilts or cushions out of your loved one's clothes. I think it's such a great idea. It's repurposing items to make them useful.

I have discussed artwork above. You can have them transformed into photo books; use a frame that is spring loaded so you can store them all in there. There is a company that puts their first handwriting on prints for you to display. I do think it is important to not get carried away with all these, though. Don't get things for the sake of getting them; think, do I really need all this?

ACTION

- Go to the library with your children.
- Choose some items to keep for sentimental reasons.

Don't try and do everything at once. This is a marathon, not a sprint. Do little by little to make it achievable.

Oh, and always take before and after photos, and post on Instagram @more_to_organising #moretoorganising, or on the Facebook page, More to Books.

Competition time – Show me craft made from junk modelling.

Notes

Notes

Chapter 8

Tidying Up

D o you remember spring cleaning? Do you still do it? Why is it only in spring? I think we should do quarterly cleans; we should call it seasonal cleans. Give everything a good dust, pull everything out, and put it back neatly, while switching out the clothes that don't fit and the clothes for the wrong season.

Habits

You're not going to like this. Decluttering and organising is an ongoing thing. It isn't a do-it-once job and then you're done. It's like fitness; you can't just go for a long run and that's you healthy for the rest of the month. It's a big bit here and a little bit there. It is a process and a journey. My journey is an amalgamation of smartening up the shoes and putting the correct sizes back on the right shelves in Clarks shoes at the Design Outlet. It was the stockroom, with stock analysis and shelf stocking in the Body Shop, twisting the bottles and colour coordinating. Then it was date checking in Marks and Spencer Food. When I was a teacher, it was organising the rooms with continuous provision so that the children could learn without being hindered, to organising children's lives with their parents in many homes, as well as helping them move houses. I finally realised I needed support for my own space when I met Suzanne Roynon, the UK's leading Interiors Therapist, because I was carrying boxes from house share to house share, never opening them from the year I moved to London and before. Sometimes, you need an outsider to help you see what's holding you back. If you support your children to do this when they are young, it will not be as difficult as it was for you or me. It will become their habit and their second nature.

I talked about the tidy up song when we were talking about bath time. There are even songs that you can put on from YouTube, which I used to use all the time as a teacher. Recently, I was singing the song to my new nanny children, and they were like, you can just tidy it all up, but then the boy wanted his name in the song, so he was on board pretty quickly. The toddler got so upset that everything had been tidied away, so her name wasn't in the song. Luckily, one piece had dropped on the floor, so she got to help tidy up! It's a team thing. I also made dens for them recently, and they really wanted them to stay up. I think that by explaining why, and making sure they know that if they help, they can have another den another day, is half the battle— explanations, expectations, and following through with it every time. Don't get a new activity out until they have helped tidy up that one; if it takes time, it takes time. Eventually, they just help without questioning. It also means things are less likely to be lost or broken.

My parents always used to clean and tidy the house before we went on vacation. I can remember sitting the wrong way on the sofa (you know, so that you feel like the world is upside down, and you can imagine having to walk on the ceiling) while my dad was hoovering, wondering if they were cleaning and tidying for a burglar to enjoy when we are away. It was so that when we came home, the house was orderly and we didn't have to do anything. I do that now. I am my parents' daughter. If all you do is clear the fridge, fruit bowl, and veg box, and take the bins out, then that's the least you can do; well done. There was one time that I put it all in a bin bag, ready to put in the bin, and then got distracted before I left; so at the beginning of the trip, I was worrying about maggots or mice, but you'll be happy to know that no mice ever did find that bag. But flies did...

Labelling

Definitely, when being a teacher and a nanny, labelling really helps, as there is more than just me in the classroom or house. Other people need to know where things are too. As I have said, children might need photographs as well as the words. Your little children are not going to be able to read yet. But actually, by putting the picture with the words, they will start to recognise what those words mean, well before they can read.

Like With Like

Placing items all together that are to do with that thing, means it's obvious where it should be stored. When organising children's bedrooms, I make sure all their hair things are next to each other, and all the stationary pieces are next to each other. I even make sure construction is in an area, and small world in another. What makes sense? If you know the batteries are stored there, then you'll know that's where you also keep the wires, because they all are to do with power. So, if someone needed a wire, it makes sense where you would go to look for an item.

Miscellaneous Box

This box is my favourite. There are just some children's items that I can't categorise. It's like the free pass of organising. But also, this box is great if you and the kids need a quick tidy up. All sorts of things can be scooped up and plopped in this box. And it isn't that it stays like this and then they end up tipping it out to find something they lost. When they have a pocket of time, perhaps when they get up at some ungodly hour, like children do sometimes, they can sort through it and put some things back in the correct, labelled box so that when they come to play again, it's all ready for them.

For bonuses go to ...

ACTION

- Set a new habit with your children and commit to it.
- Label your boxes.
- Make a miscellaneous box.

Don't try and do everything at once. This is a marathon, not a sprint. Do little by little to make it achievable.

Oh, and always take before and after photos, and post on Instagram @more_to_organising #moretoorganising, or on the Facebook page, More to Books.

Notes

Notes

Work With Me

I really hope you enjoyed this book and that you got some tips on how to organise and declutter. Remember, it has to make sense for your family, your house, and your life.

Follow me on Instagram @more_to_organising, or on the Facebook community, More to Books, which shares both organising and education.

If you'd like a little extra support, then sign up to my online course, which takes you through the areas bit by bit but with accountability.

If you would like me to come into your home, please contact me at moretobooks@gmail.com, or we can have coaching calls where I support you to clear the areas you need, with moral support and a little bit of cheerleading.

With thanks to...

I would like to thank all my nanny children (who have a huge place in my heart) and my nanny families who have made me the nanny I am today, especially Aly Samwell and Nabanita Ghosh, who have supported me so much through my journey.

Gratitude to my nanny friends that have supported me to become a better nanny, and had wisdom on things that I needed to learn; especially Sue, who has proofread this book for me, as well as having been so supportive about my blog and children's books.

Thank you to UK Nanny LTD, My Nanny Collaborative, and My Nanny Circle, which have been wonderful for networking, speaking, and being part of an international group of nannies.

To my mum for encouraging me to take the steps to live my life for me; and to my Dad, for always being proud of me.

The hugest thanks to my own interiors therapist, Suzanne Roynon, who helps me to organise my own space and my life.

A great big thank you to Deb Archibald, my coach from One of Many, who helped me get out of my own way.

Speaking of gratitude, start your day off with your children by talking about three things you are all grateful for, and about something they are looking forward to that day. When I put children to bed, or leave the house for that evening, I always thank them for a lovely day, and I always thank them for working as a team to help tidy up!

Thank you to all my decluttering clients; it really brings me joy, especially when I get to colour coordinate things. It makes my heart sing.

Love Kat x

Printed in Great Britain
by Amazon